What's wrong "big" witches . . .

… that they get caught up in all their petty little witch wars all the time and stuck in all their ego?

It's not about them. It's about getting the word out about the God and the Goddess and about service and about helping other people spiritually.

How will non-pagans ever take us seriously if we can't get our act together? What right do we have to call ourselves spiritual if we're constantly trying to hurt each other?

And damn it, I resent the time that I'm spending shielding.

There is so much other work I could be doing with that energy right now and so many better places to put my energy other than keeping nightmares away from my children ….

Current and Upcoming Books

All books in The Priestess Diaries series
stand alone and can be read in sequence
or out of sequence

Celebrating the Tower Card

A Wedding of Souls

Drink of Me

Celebrating
the Tower Card

Book #1 of The Priestess Diaries

by
Lauren Hartford

Spilled Candy Books
Niceville, Florida USA

Author's Note
and Acknowledgments

The Priestess Diaries are a novelized combination of true-life events taken from personal journals, articles, and interviews with High Priestesses, a High Priest, and spiritual leaders. Each book in the series emphasizes particular spiritual lessons and provides a context for their implementation. The series also uses the backdrop of a developing love story and its ups and downs because it is within the framework of relationships with others that we learn our greatest lessons and are given both the reason and the need to learn who we are in order to love unconditionally.

The journeys presented in this series of books are often based on the information available at the time of the story and the characters' perception of that information at that time. As more information becomes known to the characters, some of this information will be proven wrong in future stories, but it is important to present the characters' perception of truth at each phase of their development because understanding is critical to spiritual growth. Some of these flawed perceptions will be evident to the reader and observer long before they are evident to the character in the journey. Such is life.

Characters described in the series are composites of many personalities in the pagan community and any familiarity with these characters represents the universality of the human, pagan, and spiritual experiences—both very good and very bad. The characters are not always presented in positive terms, but then, these books aren't meant to be "fluffy." The characters, like real people, are flawed, fallible, and capable of redemption.

The Dragon Hart Grand Coven is not a representation of any organization with *Dragon* or *Hart* in its name. I used this word combination because of my own fondness for dragons and deer. The Grand Coven is an amalgam of over a dozen large and small groups, evidence of the joys and abuse inherent in any spiritual family. The Priests, Priestesses, leaders, and members bear the universal traits of any spiritual organization's membership, with certain elements emphasized for the purpose of demonstrating the dangers of any spiritual group becoming a cult and the "wars" that result from the need to control versus the need to be free.

Celebrating
the Tower Card

1

Early August 2004
Thursday - Full Moon in Aries, Newly Waning

"The Gods love you so much that They're willing to strip away from you everything that is illusion and replace it with something that's real."

I sit in the dark and try to meditate, but Leo's words still echo in my ears, even now—*especially* now—as my Elevation to Third Degree High Priestess of Dragon Hart Wicca approaches. Lady Dragon, my tradition's spiritual leader, warned me three years ago before I committed to a five-year course of study to become pagan clergy. If I'd known then how hard it would be, I'm not sure I would have agreed to my Initiation. I especially did not think I would be ready in a mere three years, but the changes have come hard and catastrophically, like the Tower Card of any Tarot deck.

This past year, deep within the inversion of my Second Degree abyss, has changed me in ways I can't describe.

And it's been hell, sheer hell. Saying goodbye to people I'd always thought would be in my life. Facing my codependency issues. Realizing I'd spent the past 23 years in an abusive relationship *and didn't know*. Leaving my husband to start my life over at age 42 with two young teen daughters and absolutely no intentions of ever being involved with another goddamned man.

"The clouds will part for you, at last," Leo had said, "and what you're going to see will be really ugly, but you'll see it clearly for the first time."

He was right. My divorce from Quentin is in the works, and I'm ascending from the depths. Not shattered but not untouched either. I've faced my shadow side, beamed the light on it, and dispelled the fears. I'm sick to death of illusions. I'm ready to reclaim my life now. I'm ready for something *real*.

But I'm not steady on my feet yet and I'm nervous about whether I can make it on my own. Most people don't understand. I'm a professional business woman with a high-powered career where I'm absolutely, totally confident and in-charge—the polar opposite of how I've felt in my home life. In my Government job as a consultant, I earn $80,000 a year for my base salary, yet amazingly I have no idea if I can keep a roof over my head or keep my kids from starving.

I honestly don't know what I'm worth, and I'm scared I'm worth nothing. I've been beaten down emotionally, and I've lost my confidence. I still don't know how it happened. I'm terrified I'll leap and fall, mainly because that's what I've heard all my life from my husband. Never mind my salary. I've always been told I was a financial burden on the family and should do better because my income-earning potential was my only real value to the man I loved. I see that now, but the damage has been done.

The doubts set in again, here in the dark, and I repeat to myself Leo's words:

"The Gods love you so much that They're willing to strip away from you everything that is illusion and replace it with something that's real."

Yes, Leo was right. But then, Leo's readings are usually accurate. About 98% in my case. The 2% where the discrepancies lie are easy to understand.

Sometimes he's not so perfect when it comes to exact timing. He sees things as already having happened when they're still slightly into the future, but his guides in the Ether may be to blame for that. Their time passes differently from ours and they can be in the past, present, and future all at once. For example, two years ago, when I was Initiated into the Dragon Hart Wicca Priesthood, Leo gave me my first reading and told me some specific time periods. Toward the end, he said he'd noticed I hadn't asked about the future of my job. Didn't I have any questions?

"Sure."

I didn't really. I was already reeling from his advice not to kill myself, no matter how bad things got. Leo's definitely not one of those warm-and-fuzzy types who sugarcoats his prophecies in hopes you'll send him a huge love offering and ask for a repeat performance. He'd looked a year down the road and told me that he didn't see a divorce, but he did see misery. Then he told me exactly what my husband had been up to. In excruciating, clairvoyant detail, and that I should remember that it wasn't my fault, that it had nothing to do with me, but I would suffer from it all the same.

Me? I didn't believe it, not until a few months later when every word turned out to be true. In excruciating detail that I could never have imagined. And then, just as Leo had said, I wanted to die.

"Oh, sweetness. Oh, Raven. Your husband is a very, very manipulative man," Leo had told me during that first Tarot reading at a Grand Coven gathering the night after my Initiation. Shivering, we sat under a tent canopy in the Maryland woods with only a pillar candle to cast a flickering light across the two decks of cards he threw down simultaneously on the picnic table between us. Newly Elevated Third Degrees chatted with our Grand High Priestess, Lady Dragon, sang Goddess songs all around us, danced around the campfires in the State Park, yet I barely noticed. I was too focused on Leo's words, which seemed so far-fetched back then.

I shook my head. My husband? Manipulative? But I was the one who was always wrong. At least, that's what I'd been told so many times that I believed it. Brainwashed, somehow, over the years by a verbally and emotionally abusive mate who hated my spirituality, hated my dreams of a writing career, and—it seemed—hated me. Sure, he was pissed that I'd taken a week's vacation to attend a spiritual retreat that he'd declined to accompany me on and I knew it would be hell to pay when I got home, but....

"Quent's not manipulative," I protested to Leo. "Really. When I get home, I'll ask him!"

"Oh, sweetheart...." Leo pressed his lips together in a grimace and shook his head, his long black hair tumbling wildly on his shoulders. "A couple of years from now when you're a Third Degree, you're not even going to recognize yourself."

So when Leo asked if I had any other questions, specifically ones that were career-oriented, I couldn't think. My husband had finally agreed to *let* me quit the day job I'd hated for years—the one that paid $80,000 a year in base salary—and stay home to be a full-time mom and writer as of that autumn, then he'd become sullen and hateful until I reneged, giving up a lifelong dream because I thought it was the only way I could save my marriage. Little did I know what he'd been up to! But I was back at the job I hated, back to making sure I brought in a good paycheck— the only trait of mine that my husband clearly admired—

back to trying to smile through every day while my heart was breaking and knowing I'd given up a dream.

The last question on my mind for Leo was anything about the job I hated. But clearly, Leo had something he was dying to tell me.

"Okay." I gave in. "So what's going on with my career? I just put my name on the list for a promotion—"

"Oh, honey, you're outta there!" Leo announced gleefully. He scratched at his goatee, which had a tiny splotch of blue dye in it to match the highlights in his hair. "You're already gone!"

I stared across the wooden table at him in confusion and watched the candlelight play off his features. Leo could be a great, big, ol' teddybear of a gay High Priest, and this was one of those times.

"No, that can't be right," I told him, my voice cracking. "I'm staying put. I already made the decision not to resign so that my husband wouldn't think I was selfish to follow a dream."

Leo shrugged and grinned. "They're telling me that you're already gone."

"I can't be. I'm almost guaranteed this promotion. I'm already doing the job in my office now."

"Oh, sweetness, you're out of that office. Your time there is done. The next place you work will be better to you."

"But-but when?"

"It's a done deal. You're already gone."

To me, it *wasn't* a done deal. But two months later, I interviewed for a promotion for the job I was already doing. My boss told me I'd nailed it. Just a matter of stamping the paperwork. She discreetly told me the job was mine but not to say anything yet. I'd officially have the title to go with the work I'd been doing for the past two years.

Except that someone else—someone with no experience with this type of work—got the job, and I was told I would have to train my new supervisor.

A scant four months after Leo had told me I was already gone from my then-current office, I was promoted unexpectedly into a job in another organization. A good job. A nurturing place that would be safe for me during the hell that was to come.

So Leo's guides saw an event four months into the future as the present, maybe even already passed.

That wasn't the only way Leo miscalled the future. Not only was his timing sometimes a little off, but the way he saw death was downright distressing.

"You will soon lose someone close to you," Leo told me. "It's a parental energy."

My heart skipped a beat. My verbally, emotionally, and physically abusive father had been ill for years, using each and every sickness to manipulate his loved ones into doing his bidding and hiding his recoveries. My sweet, co-dependent mother…well, I loved her beyond words.

"Not *your* parents," Leo corrected quickly. He must have seen the look on my face. "Your husband's. His mother, I think. You'll lose her within the turn of a year. Has she been ill perhaps?"

I shook my head. "Just minor stuff, but his father's just had heart surgery and refuses to give up the cigarettes. Could it be him?"

"Hmmm, maybe. No. No, definitely a maternal energy associated with him. This is his mother. Definitely his mother."

For the next year, I fretted over her impending death. Her health wasn't great and she didn't take care of herself properly, especially for a woman in her late 60's. Unlike many wives, I genuinely liked my mother-in-law. I was the lone family member she could confide in about her near-death experience as a child or visitations from the Spirit World. Too often, she braved a 110-degree summer heatwave to build a stone wall in her garden, alone, with no water and no one nearby in case of emergency. I worried about her and got into a quick habit of dropping by to visit her on my lunch hour three times a week, bringing lunch with me and a chance for her to unload her stresses. I dreaded the day when I would drive up, sweet tea in hand and chicken nuggets in a bag, and find her keeled over in the broiling sun.

It didn't happen like that.

She didn't die physically, yet in a little more than a year after that reading, she was indeed dead to me. I visited her when her facades were down and saw the real woman and not the illusion. The illusion had been lovely and polite, but I saw firsthand that day how she would turn against me once she learned her son and I were having marital problems. She told me of her daughter's husband and how she'd sweetly and faux-compassionately persuaded him to confide in her the ugly details of his marriage because she'd never tell anyone, how he'd broken down and cried like a lost toddler, how she planned to deliver every detail she got out of him to her daughter to be used against him in divorce court. Her son-in-law's trauma was only one of the dramas unveiled that day, but I saw her as she really was for the first time, with her shields down and manipulative as hell. And I realized I never really knew her at all. Just the façade of politeness and concern.

Not long after, Donna, the High Priestess and Elder who'd trained me, mentioned that Leo sometimes sees death metaphorically rather than physically. I wished I'd known that a long time ago, but even if I had, I would have been less likely to believe a time would ever come when my beloved mother-in-law would be emotionally dead to me.

But even with Leo's little idiosyncrasies in his readings, I really can't complain. Other than his timing being a little off and his maybe-literal-maybe-not view of death, he's always been right on target with his predictions for me and his insights into my life. I've met plenty of psychics over the years, mostly bad ones, but Dragon Hart Wicca does have a habit of attracting some of the best talent in the U.S. and Canada.

Here in the dark, I make a mental note to ask Leo for another reading, preferably right after my Third Degree Elevation ritual. He'll be a part of the ceremony. He'll stand and vouch for me, and I couldn't be more honored. I'm told that as soon as the ritual is over, I'll be buzzing for the next month because I'll be so infused with the power that will be passed on to me—all the way back to Gerald Gardner—that I'll believe I can walk on water. So even if Leo has bad news for me in his next reading, I either won't care or I'll tell myself that I can change everything.

It's been almost a year since his last reading. That one shocked me, even more than the previous year where he'd extracted a promise that I wouldn't commit suicide if things got really bad.

We'd been at another Grand Coven meeting, same Maryland campground but a different spot. This time, the weather was warmer. A dozen kerosene lanterns and solar-panel garden lights around the tent gave plenty of light for the double deck of Tarot cards Leo tossed onto the tarp-covered picnic table between us. Leo had just come from consecutive rituals for Third Degree candidates and it was already well after midnight. New Third Degrees laughed and sang in the distance while others munched on chips and cookies after a day of fasting. Excitement buzzed through the night air. Leo was stoked on the energies of the rituals and very attuned to the Spirit World as he began.

"Oh." Leo went still and seemed to listen for a moment. "You're divorced?"

I stopped twisting the wedding band on my finger. "No. No, but I'm seriously considering leaving him. I think I'll probably see a good lawyer as soon as I get back home from this retreat. A divorce has been iffy for almost a year, but Quentin keeps talking me into giving him another chance. We're trying to work things out and he keeps saying he's given up the porn addiction and the escort services but…but I just don't know. My gut instinct is that he hasn't."

Leo threw down a card—*Manipulation*—and then listened to voices I couldn't hear. "You'd be right. He's at it right now, as we speak. He hasn't given up anything. He's just hiding it better. The minute you get home, before he knows you're home, go right then and check the history file on his computer. Look at the Internet cookies. You'll see where he's been and who with."

I sighed and looked across the series of picnic tables at my thirteen-year-old daughter, Rhiannon, who'd accompanied me on the trip and was serenely listening to crickets in the woods and smiling to herself for the first time in years. My other daughter, ten-year-old Sonnet, had had to stay behind with her dad, much to her disappointment. If she was home with him and he was up to his old tricks….

"When you get home," Leo warned me, "your husband is going to be all sweetness and light. But it'll all be a lie. All an illusion. None of it will be real. He'll tell you whatever it takes to make you stay."

I played with the wedding band on my finger and wondered how much longer I'd be able to wear it. My husband and I were no longer sharing a bed and only once every few months, when he seemed to be trying, really trying to be supportive and loving, did we have sex. There was no lovemaking to it. No passion. Just a biological function that left me cold because I couldn't forget that I was nothing more to him than a hole in the mattress. I'd been on anti-depressants for months just to live with him, but I'd given them up when I'd discovered I was codependent. The drugs only made me more compliant and what I needed, according to my best friend Jan, was to kick his ass.

"You know," Leo continued, "I'm reading you as divorced. You're emotionally divorced already. It's all over but the legalities."

He was right, as usual. I'd known the night I'd confronted my husband about his secrets, not long after Leo's first reading the year before when he'd told me not to kill myself, no matter what. I'd known that night that our marriage was over. I'd known it by the look in Quentin's eyes. No regret. No remorse. Sheer hatred aimed at me for having found out, thanks to Leo. And then I'd run to the bathroom to throw up.

Leo plunked down two more cards, and then two more. He frowned at them and looked up at me. "I know it's been difficult for you and will be for a little while longer, but it *will* work out on every level. All this pain is for a reason." He smiled, a serenity veiling his eyes. *"The Gods love you so much that They're willing to strip away from you everything that is illusion and replace it with something that's real.*

"What do you mean?" I glanced at Rhiannon to make sure she was occupied and not eavesdropping.

"In the last two months before your divorce is final, you're going to meet someone new." Leo inhaled deeply, then let the breath escape. "And honey? He's going to be worth every second of this pain. You have to go through all of this before you can get to him."

My jaw must have hit the table. "You mean...a man?" I cringed. I didn't want a man. I just wanted my husband...and I wanted him to love me and cherish me and respect me and share with me and...and all the things he didn't do.

"Not just any man, sweetness." Leo's eyes lit up. He was seeing this mystery man in the Ether between us. "Oh, honey, he's gonna be a real *treat* for you! Really cute. And if he's got a brother, I want him."

I grinned back at Leo and promised myself I wouldn't let Leo's partner know about his amusing leer. Then my smile faded. "I'm not leaving my husband for another man."

"No, of course not. This man comes into your life just as you're finishing up all the paperwork. He's like a yummy dessert at the end of a really bad meal. He's…oh, you're going to like this one! He's really hot."

"So he's like a boy-toy? A sex toy right after my divorce?"

Leo dodged my question. "He's going to be a real treat for you. Very hot, very sexy. And honey—" Leo took a deep breath and sighed romantically— "he *so* gets you. He *totally* gets you."

I swallowed. A man who got me? A man who understood me? Impossible. I'd never had that.

"He's going to be a wonderful friend to you and you two will have a long and fruitful relationship, for the rest of your lives. Very distinguished, sorta like a young Clark Gable. Emotionally intelligent. Oh, you so deserve this! You'll travel together—he'll take you to Europe, maybe to Scotland. You're going to have so much in common. He'll be a twin flame to you, a soulmate. Everything you've been through with Quentin will be worth it to get to this man. Your marriage to Quentin will be nothing more than a bug splat on the windshield of your life. But this man? He's going to be the real thing, sweetie."

"Am I going to…marry this guy or will he be a fling or just a friend?"

"Hmmm, there's romance, yes. I see him falling for you when the moon is in Leo—no pun intended—and I see him kissing you for the first time when the moon is in Scorpio. And the first time you sleep with him, the moon will be in Scorpio."

I blinked. "Same night? Okay, so there's sex and romance. Is this a…a lasting relationship?"

"I don't know if there's marriage or not. But he's very special. A wonderful friend. He's the whole package. He doesn't have a lot of money, but he has access to a lot of money. He's smart, articulate. He's musical. Plays the guitar. And plays it exceptionally well. But no matter what you do, don't sleep with him yet. You're going to be tempted to when you first meet him but wait until your divorce is final or your soon-to-be-ex will ruin his career. There's something hands-off about him, some reason why you can't sleep with him right away, other than your ex. You can do lunch with him, but nothing more. Not yet. Just give it a little while."

"Okay. Yes. I understand." I had already decided I wouldn't sleep with anyone until the divorce was final. I didn't want to be accused of leaving my husband for another man. I wasn't. If I left him, it would be for a woman—me.

"The guy, this *treat*," I asked, "do I know him?" In spite of Leo's contrary description, I was thinking of an old flame, Scott, who'd called me recently to see if I was still married and to beg me to get out while I still could. I didn't have the same feelings for Scott, not anymore, but maybe they could be rekindled later when I was single. Still, I guess I wanted it to be Scott, so I kept trying to twist Leo's words to apply where they didn't readily.

"No, this is someone new." Leo thought for a moment. "Or you may know him but you've definitely never thought of him this way."

Okay, so that didn't sound like Scott. Still, I had to ask one more time. "Can you give me a physical description?" A young Clark Gable? Not my old flame.

"Athletic, great body, not too tall, brownish hair, blue eyes."

That might have described Scott, though I hadn't seen him in a while except for a business lunch several years ago where we'd barely spoken more than a dozen words. No silver or gray in his hair? Maybe with a little dye? I was confused. "So is he about my age, maybe a year older?"

Leo grinned. "No, this guy's younger. Much."

That stunned me. Okay, definitely not Scott. Unless Leo was seeing Scott the way he looked last time I saw him. "You're sure he's younger than I am?"

"Yeah. A lot younger. He's passed his first Saturn return. I'd say he's about 31 or 32."

I gasped, then laughed out loud. My daughter jerked her head up at the sound. She hadn't heard me laugh in a long time. "You're joking, right? I'm 41. You're saying I'm going to have a relationship with this hot, smart, musical man who gets me and is a decade younger than me?" This didn't sound real—it sounded like fantasy. One of those relationships that would be too good to be true.

"Yep. He's a widower, too." Leo paused. "Or maybe not. His wife is either dead or dead to him. I'm not sure which. But you'll have children and children in common. I hate to sound like a bad romance novel, but he's going to be *The One* for you. Five years from now, Quentin will still be just as screwed up as he is now, but you'll have a new man and a whole new life and everything will work out perfectly on every level."

"On every level," I repeated under my breath. "But I don't really want another man in my life."

Leo nodded furiously. "I know. You're going to look at this guy and be like, 'What do you want, fucker?' and he's going to be like, 'I just want to be with you.'"

No man had ever just wanted to be with me. I'd always had to earn love, often by being something I wasn't. But someone would love me just for me? I teared up. "When? This fall?"

"Within a year of your split, this new man will pop in." Leo didn't define what he meant by split—physical separation, the final divorce papers, or what. "And then when your husband comes crawling back to you, it'll be 'Quentin who?'"

I laughed again. Laughing felt good. Uncommon but good.

"That all sounds wonderful, Leo, even though I'm not exactly looking for this guy. But hey, you know what? I don't want another man who makes fun of my spiritual beliefs. Will he understand my spirituality?   Is this guy pagan?"

"No, not exactly. But he is spiritual." Leo cocked his head to listen to the voices and squinted into the Ether. "He's spiritual in a 'cowabunga, dude,' sort of way."

"What?" Okay, I certainly didn't know anyone like that. "Sure, Leo. Whatever. As long as he's not like Quentin."

"Oh, he's nothing like your husband. Or any other man you've ever known. This man will adore you and you'll adore him, and this man, he'll *want you to live.*"

I've spent most of the year since that reading trying to work things out with Quentin, discovering it was all just lies, finding more porn and escort services listed in his Internet history files, confronting him only to have him suggest that he was innocent and that our ten-year-old daughter had been the culprit, finding out he'd left an Internet history of bestiality and anal sex and fisting on the computer where our little girl had found them and been too traumatized to look any man or boy in the eyes ever since, then amazingly giving him another dozen second chances, and finally coming to realize that he'd been abusing and manipulating me for years but it had happened so gradually over time that I hadn't realized it. I've been like the frog that jumps out of hot water immediately, knowing the dangers, but slowly boils to death when the temperature's turned up only one degree at a time. I've filed for divorce, almost reconciled twice, and finally gotten him to move out, just yesterday.

Have I looked for The Treat? Yes and no. I hope I'll know for certain it's him when I meet him. Every now and then, I'll be introduced to a guy at work who's in his early 30's and attracts my interest for at least five minutes. Maybe even enough for me to think, Is that The Treat? But none of them have the appeal of the man Leo described. And besides, right now, I've had enough of men.

When I filed for divorce three months ago, I did it with the knowledge that I'll probably be alone for the rest of my life. I have no intention of dating. No plans to ever be with another man either as a lover or partner and probably not even as a friend. I just want my freedom. I want to be alone and free. I have no interest at all in men. Just in getting my life back. In reclaiming *me*.

So maybe Leo was wrong about meeting this man within two months before my divorce finalizes. Then again, Quentin's contesting everything, right down to my middle name, still trying to control me. Who knows how many more months before this nightmare is over?

As for now, I don't have time to think about a man called The Treat. I have an Elevation ritual to prepare for, and I have less than a week to be ready to start my life over as a new Third Degree High Priestess.

2

Friday - Moon in Taurus, Waning Gibbous

I slam the driver's door of my black Mercedes and hobble toward my office without looking back. I hate the Mercedes. It's so not me. I was raised on a farm in Georgia and walked barefoot everywhere I could, just to feel Mother Earth under my feet. I'm not the Mercedes type. I'm more of a pickup truck kind of girl. Or maybe an SUV. Something I can haul things in.

The Mercedes is just another reminder of the miserable life with my ex. He'd insisted I get rid of the old wreck I'd been driving and buy a new vehicle that would flaunt our financial successes. I'd said no, I'd rather drive a piece of junk and be a stay-at-home mom and writer. He'd said I could do that, too—that buying a new car wouldn't postpone my dreams—but by the time we got the new tag for the Mercedes, he'd already blown up at me, telling me we couldn't afford for me to drive a luxury car if I quit my job and that I was being selfish. That car represents my servitude to image and the surrender of my closest held dreams. I hate it. Despise it. As soon as our divorce finalizes, I'll trade it for something less pretentious…and fully paid.

I walk uphill toward my office. By now, I'm limping. People are staring. I push forward, wondering how much longer I can keep this up. I twisted both my knees eight months ago while saber fencing with a novice and haven't been able to take time off from work to take care of it. Maybe if I'd done something about it back in January instead of waiting until August, I wouldn't be in so much pain. But I didn't.

Throughout January, February, and March, I'd spent my weeks alternating between ninety hours of office work and being home too sick to crawl out of bed. The stress of my failing marriage and the impending divorce left me exhausted and vulnerable to every virus I met. By April, my pollen allergies kicked in and knocked me to the ground, and still I tried to go to work.

Hell, if I wasn't dead, I was expected to be at the office. Not by my boss. By Quentin.

Through much of April, I'd been too sick to sit up on the sofa and eat the soup the girls brought to me and yet, Quentin had demanded to know why I was staying home. He fretted over the potential loss of a day's pay, even though I couldn't possibly have driven myself to work or remained upright once I got there.

I made an appointment for a check-up and medicine and managed to drive to the clinic, which was only a few blocks from my house. I relayed my husband's demands to our family physician, Dr. Matthews, and he immediately put me on bed rest for a week. I've always liked him but for some reason, he was extremely worried about me that day. After I had to follow the doctor's orders, Quent stopped his haranguing, I got some rest, and I recovered without Quent ever once checking on me to see if I still lived and breathed.

But it was a lesson. Before then, I worried that if I didn't have Quent, who would take care of me if I got sick? My daughters answered that question for me.

Bottom line, I need to see Dr. Matthews for my knees. I didn't even mention it to him back in April. I was too sick to think of anything beyond the current illness. Work was too grueling, and then I got busy with filing the divorce papers and thinking Quent wasn't going to fight the divorce and then him changing his mind because he was certain that our marriage could be saved...now that I was gone. May, June, and July have passed and we're already into the first week of August. I've got to do something or I won't be able to walk next week at my Elevation ritual. I suppose they'll want me to *stand* to cast a circle. It's not very priestessly of me to call the Quarters while huddled on ground with an ice pack applied to my knee caps.

I've already asked Donna to inquire if they can put me in a camping spot close to the bathrooms so I won't have to walk so much. My knees are killing me right now, and I can't take time off from work until September when my workload lightens considerably. What will my knees be like in another week?

A man in a black business suit and red tie passes me on the broken sidewalk outside my building. The epitome of tall, dark, and handsome. "You all right, Miss Hartford?" His name is Ron...something. One of the VIPs from Washington. I'm surprised that he knows my name.

I nod appreciatively and push past him. My jaw is set tightly and tears run down my face, but I keep walking in my flat shoes. Even in my most comfortable shoes—even barefoot—the pain is so bad now that I cannot bend to my knees to pick up the morning paper. I can't walk up or down steps, even the single step that leads to my front door. I can't walk uphill. I can't walk downhill. I can't even lower myself onto the toilet without holding my breath against the pain as my knees bend. This morning, I was tempted to pee standing over the toilet rather than enduring the pain of sitting down. I can't keep going this way. I have to do something.

Maybe I'll do a little spell for pain relief. For whatever reason, I'm not supposed to be healed yet, and I know this. But nothing says I have to suffer!

In my office, which is rather isolated from the rest of the consultants I work with, I have a discreet altar on my desk that no one recognizes for what it really is, with the sole exception of Martin, a physicist and ceremonial magician who works with me on the occasional project when he's in town. The desk altar is a simple thing: a circle of glass "stones," a feather in the East, a river rock in the North, a red candle in the South, and a seashell in the West. In the center of the circle is a polished rock with *joy* inscribed. Whatever I put in the center is what I most yearn for, and the Joy Rock has occupied that spot for the past year. Today, I just might stand in the middle of my desk altar.

I pause at the steps leading into my building. Twenty-two of them, and there is not another way in unless I use the handicapped entrance around back and that's too far to walk. I ascend the steps sideways, one at a time, and ignore the bystanders who frown at me. It takes twenty minutes, but I reach the main entrance, drenched in sweat at eight in the morning and clutching my geode necklace for strength.

The necklace is special, but it wasn't blessed to help me with my knees. I've worn it every day for the past six months to reduce the constant stress. Four High Priestesses and Elders of Dragon Hart and Jan—my Christian witch friend— infused the geode slice with peace, tranquility, and strength to get me through the final days of my marriage and divorce. It's the kind of necklace that really doesn't look like anything special but it attracts attention every time I wear it. People just have to reach for it. Small children run to me and point at my neck, call it shiny, and ask to play with it. Even Quentin's tried to touch it, and you'd think it would repel him and maybe encourage lightning to strike him.

I draw strength from it as I limp toward my office. The phone's ringing before I can unlock my door.

"Hello?" Breathless, I fall into the chair, straight-legged to make sure I don't bend my knees and worsen the pain.

"Well, hello, sunshine! You're late for work!"

"Screw you," I tease.

"That's my sunshine! Always happy to hear from me!" Donna laughs, loud and raucous. She's an Elder in Dragon Hart, and she's been my teacher and High Priestess for the past three years, long distance from Virginia to Florida. I think she was Initiated as "Lynx" and a few people have referred to her as "Lady Lynx." I've heard her magickal name once or twice, but she doesn't use it or titles, like Lady. She's just *Donna,* and she's actually my junior by about seven years, and has a mysterious boyfriend that she refuses to talk about, saying only that one day she'll be able to explain it all but not before I get my Third Degree.

"You'll be happy to know," Donna tells me, "you passed your exam."

I sit up in my chair. "Really? You got the results?"

"Just now. Dragon herself graded it. I told her you couldn't wait any longer. You have to purchase your airfare to the Grand Coven meeting and the big Lammas ritual—that for some reason always happens after Lammas—and you have to do it by today. If you failed the test, then you shouldn't be out the ticket price as well."

I sigh. I passed. I passed! The legendary Dragon Hart exam that was supposedly five hours long was in fact closer to twenty hours long. I took two days of vacation time to finish it without Quentin knowing and mailed the stack of papers to Lady Dragon. Months have passed with nary a word. Until now.

"Aren't you going to ask about your grade?"

"As long as I passed, I don't care. I've heard no one ever gets a perfect score."

"This year, someone did."

I laugh. "I got a perfect score?" I can't believe it. There were questions on the test that hadn't been in any of the lessons, either written or oral. The only way anyone would have known the answers was by spending time face-to-face with Lady Dragon, and I lived over 1000 miles away. "A thirty-six page exam, and you're saying I got a perfect score?"

"No, *you* didn't. But someone else did this year. Your friend Butterfuck."

Butterfly? I spin in my desk chair, glad no one else is in my office suite today, and I laugh. I reach for the Joy Rock and rub my fingers over the letters.

"Butterfly aced the test? You're kidding me." Butterfly Moonbeam, or whatever the hell her current magickal name is, is the biggest fluff-bunny I know. She signs her emails with "Peace and Light to You, Oh, My Friend in the Goddess." She tries to one-up every other Second Degree's tale of woe. She—

"Oh, stop thinking competitive thoughts," Donna says with a clairaudient snicker. "You passed. That's what's important. You scored a 95, the minimum requirement. That means this time next week, you're going to be a Third Degree."

"If I'm able to get there."

"What?" Donna is suddenly serious. "What's happened? It's not that jackass you're divorcing, is it? Is it custody problems? I told you, I'll be happy to do my drop-him-in-molasses-and-freeze-him spell to slow his ass down. Won't nothing break him out of that!"

"No, that's not necessary. He moved out a few days ago. He knows I have a trip of some kind coming up and he'll keep the girls for two extra days, though he'll probably never let me forget it."

"Your knees. I'm feeling a pressure in your knees. Ouch!"

"Yeah. It's bad. I'm worried about being able to travel." I stretch my legs in front of me and note that my knees have swollen to the size of small tree trunks. They don't look like knees anymore. I can't remember if I emailed Donna about them or not.

Donna curses under her breath. I can almost see her strawberry blonde curls shaking over her frown. "When are you going to start taking care of yourself?"

"As soon as I can. I promise. I've already talked to Personnel and they say I can take off for five weeks to stay off my knees. I have the vacation time saved up. My boss agrees I can do it whenever I can schedule it. He's retiring in a few days, so it's not like he cares anymore."

"Okay then." Donna sounds tentative. She's heard excuses from me before. "I'm worried about you."

"Don't be. I understand why I'm having these problems with my knees. Think about it from a metaphysical viewpoint." I bend and flex one knee cautiously and hear a grinding that sounds like bone on bone. I wince at the noise. "The whole situation with my husband has brought me to my knees. Get it? Or, if you prefer, I've been on my knees for far too long and now I'm ready to get up off them."

"Yeah, yeah, yeah," Donna agrees.

We've discussed it before, how metaphysical problems can manifest as physical health problems. Nausea, for example, may be from a sense of rejection. Throat problems can occur from having to swallow too much or from an inability to speak up. Even Leo, a year ago, had foretold an upcoming medical crisis for me, one in my first and second chakras, where my body would be expelling something not long after my divorce. He suggested that maybe it was constipation from feeling "stuck" in my marriage for so long or maybe irritable bowel syndrome from the need to get rid of all the shit I'd held in. Neither sounded very appealing to me at the time, and he'd frightened me by suggesting the pain would be excruciating, bad enough that I would think I was dying but that I should know that I wouldn't, that I'd be okay. But my divorce is hopefully within a few months of being finished, and the pain in my lower chakras hasn't happened yet.

"Are you doing any kind of magickal work for healing? Do you want me to gather the Elders and send you some healing energy? With your permission, of course."

"No!" The word comes out more emphatic than I'd intended. "Don't do anything."

"Remember when I was saying to take care of yourself? You know, there's nothing manipulative or unethical or inherently wrong with asking the Goddess for healing for yourself."

"That's not it. And it's not that I don't want healing. I think there's a purpose behind this injury and I'm accepting whatever it is."

"Yeah, there's a purpose. Of course, there's a purpose. What do *you* think it is?"

I suspect Donna is doing her clairvoyant thing again and ignore it. "Several things. First of all, I just got a notice of all the papers I have to provide to Quent's lawyer as part of the legal discovery process. It's huge. I mean, huge! My lawyer and I let him off the hook with some of the things he was supposed to give us. So he can provide summaries of his accounts and the yearend amounts rather than monthly bank statements and credit card bills for the past three years. Unfortunately, when we asked for the same consideration, his lawyer agreed and Quent refused. He wants to see everything. Not that he thinks I'm hiding anything, but it'll take another couple of months just to get copies from the banks. So far, I have four six-inch binders of bank statements and employer accounts that were easy to find."

"That's…a lot. I think it would take half an hour for me to get my info together. But then, you're…well-off." There's a touch of something in her voice. Bitterness? Hurt? When her husband died, he left her well-off, too, but she'd given away most of it, much of it to Lady Dragon's charities, and she'd had to go back to work full-time as a sound engineer for a small studio she co-owned with her brother-in-law to make ends meet.

I nod, though Donna can't see it. Sometimes I feel bad, guilty, about the money I earn and the wealth I've acquired, even though I've worked many, many hours of overtime. Spiritual people aren't supposed to have an interest in money, right? And being a Pisces with Pisces Rising, I have a tendency to give away much of my income, enough so that I run my pagan home business as a charity, sinking any profits back into my "Goddess work."

"It's not so much the financial statements as it is the aggravation," I tell Donna. Quent has nothing to do these days but think of ways to convince me to drop the divorce proceedings, and meanwhile, I'm so swamped, I don't have time to breathe. "He wants all the financial information on my little company. Every snippet of information, including receipts, pay stubs, and confidential mailing lists of my pagan customers—which I will absolutely not give him."

The tough part that really peeves me is that Quent agreed not to ask for information on my small pagan-oriented business, the one I run at home in my spare time that barely breaks even, the one he's never been emotionally or financially supportive of because it's related to my religion and he's an atheist who doesn't believe in anything but the Almighty Dollar. He's told me via his lawyer that he doesn't want balance sheets or tax records that show summaries. He wants printouts of every transaction and every scrap of paper.

"Just say the word," Donna tells me, "and I'll turn him into a toad."

I stifle a laugh. "You're too late. He's already a toad."

"You know what I mean. You know I don't mind working with the dark stuff. That dropped-in-molasses-and-frozen-spell will stop anything. I'll do it for you. I'd *love* to do it for you."

"Thanks, but I'll take care of it myself."

"You sure? 'Cause sometimes, I still feel like you're protecting him. Like Karma's just waiting to kick him in the balls, but you're still not wanting anything really bad to happen to him. Let it, Raven. Let it."

I don't respond. She may be right. In spite of all the hurt I've endured, I'm not angry at him. Donna has said the anger will come. Jan says it almost every day. So does Lisa. And Josie. And Belinda. But maybe I feel anger as hurt because I don't wish him ill will. All I want is for him to be gone and let me be free and let me have my life back. Well, to let me have a life. Period.

"So anyway," I continue, steering the subject back to my knee injury, "I think I'll take off the five weeks I've talked to my boss about and use that time to finish up my divorce paperwork so I can get that whole process over with. And I'll stay off my knees during that time, too. Plus...."

"What? I hear strategy in your voice. What have you got planned?" Donna herself sounds delighted.

I pick up a pen from my desk and start doodling rune symbols on my blotter. *Kenaz*, primarily. The symbol for insight and clarity. It's time to let Donna know my surprise. "As of today, I've started writing again."

Donna lets out a hoot. "That's...that's wonderful. I thought you'd given it up."

"I did. I lost all desire to write over the past couple of years, but it's back. And it's full of passion. And it wants to be let out of the bag!"

We laugh together. I doodle a pair of words—THE TREAT—without realizing what I've written.

"So I've talked to my old editor in New York, and she still wants to see a new book from me."

I've tried this so many times before. I sold a book ten years ago that hit the bestseller lists under a pseudonym, but I couldn't find time to write novels and work eighty-hours a week at my day job and so I let my writing career fizzle. Quent had been supportive enough to ask how many books I'd need to sell on a regular basis to match my $30,000 income. He hadn't seen any reason for me to stay home as a full-time mom and writer when I could do both and still work eighty hours a week. Then he'd agreed two years ago to letting me quit my day job. But that fizzled, too. He stopped talking to me for two months while I worried and wondered if our marriage would survive my decision to stay home. I'd been desperate to save my marriage. So I went back to work.

At one point, I had enough vacation time saved that I could combine it with a three-month leave of absence and finish my then-current manuscript, write two three-chapter proposals for sequels, and sell the trilogy. Then that sale would replace my day job income for long enough for me to get the book sales going and switch to writing full-time without a dip in our household income. Quent nixed that idea. We'd be without my income for three months and that, he'd said, wasn't fair to him. My dream shouldn't interfere financially with our lifestyle, even for a few months.

"Oh, my Gods," Donna says. "You're going to take your five weeks and write like a demon, aren't you?"

"Precisely!" I beam and outline two words on my blotter. Beneath them, I scribble more of my wish.

THE TREAT

I WANT TO BE HEALED

"I can't finish the book," I tell her, "but I can finish at least one really good proposal I think I can sell. If I'm lucky, two."

"Didn't you try this before? A month-long sabbatical?"

"Yeah. I saved my vacation time and told Quent I was going to stay home for one whole month and write like crazy to make my dream come true. It seemed logical to me because it meant I could have what I so badly wanted and it wouldn't mean any loss of income for the family. Not even a smidgen of a dip."

Donna curses under her breath. "I remember. He bitched you out for being inconsiderate and spending your vacation time on yourself. So you never did it. But Raven!" She inhales and lets it out slowly as she repeats my magickal name. "Raven, now you can take off for a whole month without worrying about what he'll think! As if you should ever have had to ask for permission anyway."

"Right. And the folks here at work can't say anything because I'll be home getting my knees fixed. See? I think the Goddess is using this knee injury business to force me to stay home so I can take care of business."

Donna doesn't say anything.

"Hello? You still there?"

"I'm here. It's just…I think there's more to it than you think. The knee injury is definitely fated, but for more reasons than you know."

"Like what?" I scribble to myself as I wait for her to answer.

I WANT HEALING.

I WANT TO BE HEALED.

SEND ME A HEALER.

"I don't know, Raven. Just a feeling. There's more to it, that's all. Something with far-reaching implications."

"Oooh, sounds ominous." I pick up a red pen and begin to fill in the outline of THE TREAT on the blotter. "Well, whatever happens, I know it's supposed to. So I'm not complaining about my knees. They'll be healed when there're supposed to be."

"And speaking of things happening when they're supposed to…." Donna's voice trails off as I press the phone to my ear. "Dragon reminded me that you're supposed to complete a 'Third Degree challenge' before your Elevation. She was going to give you one, but I knew how stressed you've been with the divorce and I think that just screwing up your courage to the point of being able to kick the bastard out qualifies for meeting any challenge I've ever heard of. Dragon disagrees. I don't want you having to put together a research project in the next week. No telling what kind of assignment she'd dream up and she doesn't work outside the home like you and I do. So I'm going to give you a different challenge so Lady Dragon will be satisfied that you've checked off that box and you can get your Elevation."

"You're scaring me," I confess. Last time we talked, Donna told me she considered my challenge to have been met and that I didn't need to worry about it. Now Lady Dragon didn't think my divorce was a big enough deal? Maybe not for some people!

"You don't always have to complete your challenge before your Elevation. Sometimes you're allowed to finish it within six months after the power is passed to you, but you won't get the full effect until you've finished the challenge."

I want to protest, but I know better. Lady Dragon's decisions don't always make sense to me, but she's the High Priestess of the Grand Coven and what a High Priestess says, goes. Apparently, I have to have some kind of challenge other than getting through the dissolution of my marriage and the major life change that comes with it.

"Here's your challenge: as soon as you are done with the ritual and get your Third, you must decide whether to stay with the Dragon Hart Grand Coven or leave."

I don't understand. Is she kidding? Giving me a challenge that's a no-brainer? Why would I leave? It's not that I feel close to Lady Dragon—I don't. I've met her only twice and she's said no more than a dozen words to me, ever. I'm not even sure she knows I exist. I'm much closer to Donna and all the Elders.

People don't just leave Dragon Hart Grand Coven on a whim. And especially not right after their Elevation ritual. They take a vow to train others in the name of The Morrigan and Her consort, Herne. They start their own circles and covens and teaching groups. They don't just *leave*.

"I'm staying!"

My face is hot, stinging. I drop my pen to my desk. Something's coming and it's bad. Upsetting. Shake-me-to-my-foundation serious. Donna isn't teasing or trying to give me an easy out in regards to the challenge. She's talking about a real challenge. A Tower Card kind of event.

"Donna, I already made that decision when my friend Belinda left Dragon Hart right before my Initiation two years ago. I had a chance to go with her new Grand Coven, but it didn't feel right. I knew the Goddess wanted me to stay with Dragon Hart and get my training there. I would never—"

"I'm not asking you to make a decision right now. I want you to wait until you get your Third. I know that with Belinda, you chose where the Goddess led versus leaving with your friend, and I know you'll go where the Goddess leads this time, too. Either way, I'll understand, but it *is* your decision and yours alone to make."

"But Donna, why would I ever think about leaving Dragon Hart?"

"Because," she says, her voice dropping low, "I am. We've been waiting for you. All the Elders and I are leaving just as soon as you get your Third."

3

Monday - Moon in Gemini, Waning Crescent

Lisa dabs her mouth with her oversized napkin, then toys with her low-carb lunch. Behind her vintage Gloria Steinem glasses, she's avoiding my eyes. "I got a call from Tammie."

"And?"

I haven't heard from my most timid student in almost two weeks. Neither Lisa nor Tammie have been officially dedicated into Dragon Hart Wicca but both plan to just as soon as I receive my Third Degree later this week, most likely at the Harvest Moon with a huge bonfire and an abundance of no-carb and low-carb food. Lisa, who's in her mid-thirties and takes her super-feminist fashion very seriously, has already asked to be the first member of the RavenHart Coven. Tammie, a younger and newer member of the teaching circle I started earlier in the year, immediately asked to be the second Initiate. My other three students, all of whom are pushing forty, have not yet decided if they want formal training or if showing up at my house once every four weeks for an afternoon workshop and ritual is more than enough to satisfy their spiritual thirsts. And then there's Josie, my Goth-pagan friend from work who dates a private investigator and who "isn't into group things" but wants me to work with her privately, particular with the Dark Goddess.

Now I'm not quite sure what to do. Donna's asked me to make a decision about staying or leaving the Dragon Hart Grand Coven. If I leave—and I don't know why I would—then my coven won't be officially a Dragon Hart coven and they will have to get that specific training elsewhere, most likely by asking to have a different High Priestess assigned to teach them. If I had already Initiated them, then the matter would be even stickier. As it is, now I owe not only Donna an answer, but if I leave the Grand Coven, I will also owe an explanation to my students who might prefer to train for the clergy within the auspices of Dragon Hart Wicca.

I decide to keep quiet about this to Lisa and Tammie until after my Elevation. I want to be sure.

Lisa looks uncomfortable. "Tammie's gone back to Kentucky to stay with her parents for a while. She and her husband are having some problems."

"Oh," I say, pretending I don't already know through at least thirty lunch hours of counseling sessions over sweet tea and chef salads at a local pizza place that's affordable for both of us. Tammie's as codependent as I have been most of my life, and her husband is as verbally abusive to her as Quent has been to me. She's finally figuring out what she wants in life and making a plan to go after it. I'm proud of her progress, but a little taken aback that she left town without telling me.

"She'll be back," Lisa assures me, pausing to down a teaspoon of organic apple cider vinegar she brought with her. She makes a face and contemplates the steamed vegetables on the plate in front of her. Lisa's down to a size 4 and will, no doubt, tell me more about her diet than I ever want to know and how it's a lifestyle, not a diet, and how I, too, could be a size 4 if I exercised my willpower. "Tammie just needed some time away. She wasn't going to tell any of us but…well, I have The Gift, you know."

Yes, Lisa has gifts. What she doesn't say is more important than what she does say. Lisa has psychic gifts, and I don't. Yet I'm to be her teacher.

I'll admit, there have been times when I've felt deficient. A High Priestess should be able to do everything, right? Psychic abilities, visions, Tarot reading, healing, actually seeing the electric outline of the circles you cast, just about anything you can think of. Except that I don't have what Lisa calls "The Gift of Knowing," which she received out of the blue several years ago. And I don't have what she calls "The Gift of Healing," which has come more recently.

Lisa has an uncanny ability to touch someone, absorb their pain, and then set it free. I've seen her use it five times now, each time in *circle* with my group. The first time was a surprise, but with each repeat, she becomes more confident. I've seen her take away chest pains and close emotional wounds. She's proud of her gift, almost as much as she is of her hellion-child daughter who's visiting GrandMom today and her blissful marriage to a Tarot-reading, ceremonial magician who's also a psychiatrist at a local hospital.

I don't have the healing gift. I have wished for it many times, especially when my friend Jim was dying of cancer. I wish I had it, but I don't.

Then again, there's no prerequisite out there that says that every coven leader must have certain gifts or they're not worthy of teaching. I like to think that we all have different sorts of gifts, some more amplified than others, and that we can share those gifts with each other. Maybe I can't heal and maybe I can't read a Celtic Cross spread worth a crap for anyone but myself, but I have other gifts, amazing gifts, including being able to bring together certain groups of people for certain purposes. I'm proud of those gifts, and I refuse to feel second-rate if I don't possess every possible gift in the High Priestess handbook.

Besides, I prefer to think of myself the way Donna explains it: *I'm not so much a teacher as I am a facilitator. It's Spirit that does the teaching. I'm just a go-between.*

"By the way," Lisa continues, raising a critical eyebrow as I bite into my ham and cheese croissant, "I want to take my formal Initiation at Samhain. You'll have your Third by then, and that'll mark a year and a day since I told you I wanted to Initiate."

I smile at her, pleased. I'd told her I wanted to know when she felt ready. "Of course. But keep in mind that Wicca may not be for you. Or that a tradition other than Dragon Hart may be a more intimate path for you."

She frowns, misunderstanding. She thinks I'm saying no. I'm not.

"You know, Lisa, even though a formal degree program calls for Initiations and Elevations through a directed process, it's Spirit that takes you through the steps, with or without a High Priestess to help you along. The progress I've seen you make in the last year? I'd say you're already going through the equivalent of your First Degree. You know, learning about your gifts, attuning to the Goddess, that sort of thing. You don't have to be in a coven to work through the stages, but I do think it helps to have a High Priestess to support you through the process."

She nods emphatically. Her granny glasses slide down her nose and she shoves them back into place. "I want to be a High Priestess. Third Degree. I need to be if I'm going to use my healing gift." Before I can quiz her on why she needs to be clergy to heal, she adds, "Especially if we're going to run a non-profit healing center."

Ah, the healing center. The Center of Light. Yes. We've talked about it so many times in the past year. Ever since Lisa and I ran into each other at a sword and dagger booth at a Renaissance Faire, we've shared our identical visions for a building for non-traditional healings, spiritual workshops, a metaphysical library, nature preserve, psychic readings, and even yoga classes and a little kindergarten for pagan children. I envision small dormitories on the premises where traveling teachers and healers and artists can stay for free for a week at a time while they earn their keep by teaching. I hope for a curriculum where students of Wicca, Neo-Wicca, and various forms of paganism can buy lessons and other resource material cheaply over the Internet to hone their special gifts or broaden their knowledge. I dream of—

"Crows," I whisper, squinting through the café's window across the parking lot to the medical clinic I patronize and to the neighboring fast food place I frequent once a day for a to-go breakfast biscuit to be wolfed down on the way to work. "Have you ever seen so many crows?"

Lisa laughs and cocks her head to follow my gaze. There must be several dozen birds circling the parking lot over a convertible silver Porsche. The man in the driver's seat looks familiar. Something about him reminds me of the guy who plays Mal on *Firefly*, the science-fiction western TV series written by Joss Whedon. Or maybe a shorter-haired version of *The Return of the King's* Aragon. Yeah, maybe. But younger than Viggo Mortensen.

He parks, head back as he observes the crows, his hand over his eyes to shield the sun or perhaps from the crows themselves. They light, finally, in the pines above the building, on the building, on the safety rail to the employee entrance.

Crows. Why are there so many crows over the clinic? Why the overwhelming abundance of this particular animal totem? Are they telling me to pay attention? To go

ahead and make an appointment for my knees? Right
now?

"Cute guy," Lisa says. Then her eyes widen.
"Don't tell my husband I said that."

I shrug. Why would I? She's right—the guy is
cute—but it's just an observation. She hasn't mentioned
anything about wanting to jump his bones.

"My mate and I have the most amazing connec-
tion," Lisa continues as if to defend the fact that she's human and can appreciate a good-looking man.

I know what she's going to say next. I could recite it
with her, word for word. Instead, I watch the parking lot
through the plate glass windows of the café. The man in
the Porsche is still there, tinkering with something in the
passenger seat. One last crow circles overhead and lands
on the handrail near the clinic entrance a few feet away
from him.

"Raven, I just pray that one day you'll find a love
like ours. My mate and I, we're a unit. We function as one
person. I know you never had that with Quent."

I nod. I've heard it all before. Many times. *Many.*

The man in the Porsche looks familiar. Where do I
know him from? His brown hair is a little long on top, almost in his eyes. But I can't see anything more of him than
the back of his head. Lisa has a better view, but she's trying not to look.

"No," I murmur. "Never with Quent."

Lisa leans forward across the table, her blouse skim-
ming the steamed vegetables on her plate. "If you want, I'll
take your palm and press it to my bosom."

"What?" I jerk my head up. Did I just hear her
right?

But she's completely serious. "Well, to my heart.
You should know what it's like to have the kind of love
and joy and inner peace that my mate and I have for each
other. If you want, I'll press your hand to my heart and let

you feel what it's like to have that joy so you'll know when the right man comes along." She smiles serenely, meaningfully, and then with her right hand, she holds her left hand to her heart as a surrogate for mine. "I have that gift, too, you know? To share my joy with others."

I shake off the image she wants to impart and glance again out the window. The man in the Porsche now stands over the car, sunglasses on and head lowered, punching something into his cell phone. His back is to me but he's slim with an athletic build. Nice clothes. A sort of business casual, but not the expensive stuff. I have no desire for a boyfriend or even a date right now, given the state of my divorce and my lack of trust in men, and especially not one who doesn't look a day over thirty, but Lisa's right: this man is very attractive.

"When you're ready to date again, I know a couple of men you might be interested in. Daniel. Jackson. Luke. Daniel—his friends call him Thor—used to be in Special Ops in the military. Jackson may be bisexual, if that's okay— "

I don't say anything but make a face. Quent had way too many gay friends who "kept up appearances" with unsuspecting wives. I had no qualms about the bisexuality issue, but the deception was more than I could handle.

"And Luke's about your type. I could invite them to my Samhain party and let you pick."

"No thanks."

"Well, you think about it. You're not getting any younger. Samhain's a good two months away. Luke, one of the men I'm thinking of, works with my husband at the hospital. His wife died a few years ago, and we've been trying to get him to get back into circulation."

Something clicks in my head. Something Leo said. I turn slowly back to Lisa. "He's a widower?"

"Yeah. Is that a problem?"

Leo had said that The Treat's wife was dead, or dead to him. "Does he have kids?"

"Yeah. Two. Not quite as old as your kids. He's about 35. Quite a bit younger than you."

I laugh, which leaves a confused expression on Lisa's face. "Do you know if he plays guitar?"

She frowns. "No idea. Why? Do you want me to find out?"

I shake my head. I'm not ready for another man in my life. I have too much to do right now. An Elevation to prepare for. A divorce to get through. Still, the idea of The Treat being a real person is intriguing.

"The Gods love you so much...."

The man in the parking lot pockets his phone, reaches into his passenger seat, and extracts a white shirt. No. A lab coat. He swings his long arms into it and adjusts the shoulders. It's tight on his upper arms where his muscles bulge. He tugs at the sleeves, then gives up. A split second later, he grabs a brown paper bag from the front seat. Lunch from the burger place down the street.

In three quick bounds, he reaches the employee entrance to the clinic. He waves one arm with a flourish and the crows scatter to the winds. Looking up at them, he grins, and at last I see his face.

"I think that's my doctor," I say, maneuvering for a better look. A dump truck passes outside and by the time it's gone, so is he. "Last time I saw him back in April, he had a crew cut. I need to make an appointment to—"

Lisa lets loose a little belch. She's mortified and excuses herself quickly to the restroom, explaining that it's a side effect of her new diet. I hardly notice.

Dr. Matthews. I like this man. He's been gentle with my kids, and he's treated me for repetitive stress injuries three or four times and at least once for allergies when he put me on bed rest against Quent's wishes. He's married to some stunningly beautiful woman in her twenties—I've seen their wedding photos on his desk—and he is one of the few non-pagans here in the Bible Belt to recognize the true meaning of my pentagram jewelry and talk intelligently about it. He always spends twenty or thirty minutes with me in an office appointment, quickly dispensing a prescription or diagnosis and the rest of the time chatting about Wicca and the advantages of matriarchal societies. He knows more about my religion than most people around here. Is his wife pagan? I've wondered several times, not because I've ever met her but because of his regard for women and the Goddesss. Maybe the two of them might be interested in attending one of my mind-body-spirit workshops or a spiritual gathering at my house. They'd fit in well with the rest of my group.

I fish my cell phone out of my purse and call the clinic. It's an easy number to remember, and I've been calling it for the past decade, since two doctors prior to this one. The receptionist answers on the fifth ring.

"I can get you tomorrow afternoon," she tells me.

"You don't have anything any sooner? Maybe work me in? He's done that before for me. My knees are really hurting."

"Sorry. Everybody loves Dr. Matthews. He's gotten so popular that it's hard to get an appointment with him unless you know a month in advance that you're going to be sick. The hospital we work for won't let him refuse new patients. Fortunately, someone cancelled about five minutes before you called, so he has an opening if you want it, but in another five minutes, it'll be gone."

I quickly give her my insurance information and agree to the date and time—tomorrow—which is two days before I fly to Maryland. If I can't get in to have my knees checked on before my trip to the Grand Coven meeting, I'm not sure I'll be able to walk then. How interesting that an appointment just cancelled before I called. Clearly, the Gods are at work here.

I close my cell phone and drop it back into my purse as Lisa returns. She looks a little pasty but smiles nonetheless.

"I should probably tell you," she says as she slides into the seat across from me, "that I may have injured an old friendship by deciding to be your student."

All I can do is blink at her. Then finally, I find the words and stutter, "What do you mean?"

"You met BetZ, right?"

I think for a minute, then remember. BetZ was at Lisa's Beltane party three months ago, shortly before I filed for divorce. She was exceptionally cool toward me, and it wasn't just because her lesbian lover found reason no less than three times to touch my face or my hair. BetZ is a well-known local High Priestess, but I'm not sure which tradition she follows or if her coven is eclectic. She's set herself up as a community spokesperson and every time the local newspapers want to talk to a "real witch," they give her a call. At 45 and with silver hair to her waist and a penchant for cleavage-baring black dresses, she looks every bit the part.

"Yeah, I met BetZ."

"You know BetZ's a High Priestess, too, right? Third Degree."

"Yes."

"We've been friends since we were little girls." Lisa pauses to let the information sink in. "She asked me several years ago to join her coven. It's one of the most prestigious covens in the State of Florida, you know?" She waits for me to nod, but I don't. "Anyway, I told BetZ years ago that if I ever Initiated, I'd do it with her."

Still, I don't say anything. I've never heard this particular story before, though I have heard her complain about BetZ always wanting to borrow money from her and how BetZ has a $3,000 ritual robe but can't pay her electricity bills. I'm surprised that Lisa would have considered joining BetZ's group but on the other hand, I'm not surprised at all. She's been closely involved with the group for years. Joining them would have been a natural progression.

"So I told BetZ last Yule that I was thinking of joining your coven when you got your Third. She was hurt. Bad. I reminded her that I have The Gift of Knowing and I *know* that I'm supposed to be your student. There's something you have to teach me that I can't get from anyone else. But she told me later that she'd thought about it and understood. I'd met a really great teacher who could help me with my gifts and that was more important than her ego. So BetZ was excited about the Beltane party at my house because she wanted to meet this fantastic Priestess who'd stolen me away from her."

I study Lisa as I finish my croissant. She has a habit of being blunt. Sometimes I admire that but suddenly I don't. Sometimes her affinity for "just being honest" borders on cruelty. I've never attempted to steal Lisa or anybody else. I'm simply here if someone is looking for a teacher. I still believe the old adage that says when the student is ready, the teacher will appear.

Lisa pokes at her beans with her fork and makes a face. "It's too bad you had to bring Quentin to the party. The energy in my house was fouled for a week afterwards. I had to burn Nag Champa non-stop to get rid of his vibes."

Her words cut deeply. I know how she values the purity of the energy in her home. Only certain people are allowed beyond the threshold, and if someone negative gets through or turns negative once inside, she conducts major week-long house cleansings to get the balance back to what feels right to her. I feel guilty enough for what had happened that night but Lisa specifically said I could bring Quent and the girls. Neither of us ever thought he'd accept the invitation.

Quent had been at his most controlling the last week of April, accusing me of spending too much time with our daughters and not enough time with him. He refused to be reminded that the reason Sonnet woke with night terrors every single night was a direct result of the things she'd seen at his favorite Internet sites. The more he lost control over me, the more controlling he became. If I went to the grocery store alone, he would accuse me of excluding him until I went shopping with him in tow, all the while with him grousing about how long I was taking and which foods were off-limits to the girls and me because he thought my food choices were unhealthy. If I put a low-carb product in the grocery cart, he'd take it out and replace it with a high-carb, low-fat product, even though my metabolism falls into a slumber if I eat pasta. In a year, I've gained thirty pounds eating the same foods he does.

Normally Quent hates my friends, whether they're pagan or not. He still doesn't recognize Jan on the street, and she's been my best friend for over a decade. But he especially hates my pagan friends, even though he'd never met any of them before the Beltane party. He's always referred to them as my "cult," and expressed his concern for me that I'm too stupid to know the difference between a cult and a real church, even though he's an atheist himself and has never attended church except to argue the superiority of his beliefs.

So when I mentioned that I would be attending Lisa's May Day party with the girls, he flipped that proverbial on-off switch and turned suddenly nice, telling me how much he wanted to meet my friends and understand my religion. Okay, so since then I've come to realize that he was trying to gather information to use against me to control me.

The party surprised him. First of all, no naked pagans running around. And no booze. A few chain-smokers who like to ground by sucking in air, but they all went outside on the front lawn to smoke. Only one guest showed up with a visible tattoo or piercings more extreme than in her the earlobe. No drugs. No fucking on the floor or on the stairs or anywhere in the house or yard.

The party was actually dull by the standards of his social group. He'd been surprised by the number of engineers, scientists, and teachers present and that the most daringly dressed of anyone was the host in his bright green tie.

But I was the one who'd been different. The girls had noticed and had told me. I'd worried the whole evening that he would make a scene, that something would make him unhappy. I went out of my way to try to please him, and even though he'd promised to participate in our ritual—which we based on the outlandish "Chocolate Ritual" and "sacrificed" a chocolate Easter Bunny—he instead sat on the sidelines and glowered, every five minutes looking at his watch and tapping it, even though the party had started at five o'clock and it wasn't even seven yet. Eventually, he relaxed and enjoyed himself, but I didn't. I was on guard all night, fearing what he might say to insult my friends.

"Yeah," Lisa says, "I think I lost a lot of credibility with BetZ. After you and Quentin and the girls left, she pulled me aside and said, 'What the hell are you doing? She's not Priestess material!'"

I jerk my head up. One of the things I learned early on in my study for the clergy is that you never ever question someone else's path or their elevation. At least, not within Dragon Hart. Lady Dragon's been very clear about that. Questioning can get you kicked out. You never know what the other person has been through to achieve that Elevation.

"And then BetZ said, 'How could you turn me down for *that?* I demand you answer me.' And I told her, 'I don't have to answer you. I'm supposed to be her student and it's not for me to question and it's certainly not for you to question.'"

I stop chewing and swallow. The last of the croissant sticks in my throat. Barbara, one of the Dragon Hart Elders, once told me that you have to get through all your lessons to become a High Priestess because once you start your own coven, they'll expect you to have your act together. If you don't, they'll eat you alive.

I am being eaten alive.

"That was before I left Quent. Before I understood that I had been abused all these years. Dominated. I know the difference now."

"But you're still codependent."

I nod. "And I'll always have those tendencies. It's part of my daily struggle. Maybe in a few years, they'll fade. Being a High Priestess doesn't mean I'll be perfect, Lisa. I'll just have more tools to live my life with."

Lisa shrugs. We finish our meal in silence, then throw several dollars on the table for a tip.

We say goodbye at the door of the café. I start to give Lisa a hug, but she holds up one hand to tell me no. She doesn't want to mix her energies with mine right now. Maybe after I've been away from Quent a little longer, but for now, there's too much negativity attached to me and she can't afford to pick up those bad energies. All I can do is nod my understanding. Lisa's sensitive like that.

I duck into the post office next door to check my mail before heading back to work. My personal mail, using my mundane name, goes to my home address, but I have a P.O. Box for mail related to my home business and anything pagan so that Quent won't get into it. My box is unusually full today. I pull out several invoices and orders and then a thick brown envelope.

I feel the buzz of energy on it as I touch it. My magickal name is written in tight cursive across the front. There is no return address, but the postmark is from Lady Dragon's hometown over 1000 miles from here.

My Third Degree exam? It could be. The package is thick, daunting. I'm eager to see if Lady Dragon made any comments in the margins or what she thought of the rituals I wrote specifically for the test. She compiled other

Third Degrees' rituals into a book last year and sold it on eBay to raise money for one of the Grand Coven charities, so I fully expect that she'll do the same with my rituals once she has enough fodder for a new book. She hasn't asked for permission, so maybe not.

I tear into the package and pull out a stack of papers. The smell of cigarette smoke and dragon's blood incense stings my nostrils. This isn't my exam, but I have a gut feeling it's my *test*.

These are copies of emails from Lady Dragon to the Elders of the Grand Coven and copies of messages back to her. Bank statements. Receipts. Letters of dismissal to former Elders. Investigations into new members.

Including me.

Things I'm not meant to see.

Things Lady Dragon doesn't want me to know.

4

Tuesday - Moon in Gemini, Waning Crescent

I have an appointment with Dr. Matthews one hour ago, I'm waiting impatiently but fully clothed in a slightly warm exam room with a window to the East that's too high to see anything out of but clouds, and my normally low blood pressure is sky high.

What can I say? I've been stressed. Quent is up to his old tricks again, this time trying to make the girls pity him so they'll ask to live with him full-time. My knees hurt so bad that I can barely put one foot in front of the other. Two tropical storms named Bonnie and Charley, likely to become hurricanes, are brewing in the Atlantic and heading toward Florida. And in two days, the day at least one storm is to make landfall, I board a plane for an Elevation ritual that might lead to my leaving the Dragon Hart Grand Coven. I don't know yet. I just don't know.

I can't believe the things I've read. I don't even know who sent the package, but it was someone who wanted me to see a side of Lady Dragon that I didn't know existed. And someone who was afraid enough of speaking up and being found out. The material I'd read was confidential...and disturbing.

It's crossed my mind that it might have come from Quent, except that he'd never have access to this kind of information. Not even a private investigator could have dug up this kind of dirt. This...this was from the inside, close to the throne, so to speak. When I told Donna about the package, she'd gotten uneasy, but she swore she had nothing to do with it. As an Elder, she'd taken an oath to do nothing against the High Priestess unless Lady Dragon proved herself incompetent, either mentally or morally. That's what the Elders had been for the past twenty years—a check and balance in the system so that that no one person had too much power or responsibility when it came to running the organization. But clearly from the papers I'd read, the failsafe had failed. The Elders, as powerful witches as they are, are terrified of their mentor.

I hear a rustle of papers and a knock at the exam room door. A petite nurse with bleached blonde hair and a name tag that says "Trisha" sticks her head through the crack and smiles. "Dr. Matthews is running late. He'll be with you in a few minutes. He's doing a procedure down the hall." And then she's gone.

With a nervous laugh, I rub my knees in clockwise circles. I don't know why I rub my knees now except that it feels comforting to the pain. I've already waited an hour and I know it'll be even longer before Dr. Matthews walks in. He's never on time but once he gets here, he's always worth the wait. Contrary to how I feel with my dentist, Dr. Matthews has a soothing way of lowering my blood pressure during stressful visits.

I first met Dr. Matthews around four years ago, and I've raved about him ever since. Quent even quit his regular physician, noting that he was going to see my "hot doctor." I'd thought that was strange. I'd never referred to

Dr. Matthews as *hot.* Quent had, but not me. Even if the doctor *is* hot…. I'd spoken only of his bedside manner and the way he doesn't push patients through in two minutes without listening to a word they have to say. But apparently, even a kind mention of anything was enough to make Quent green with jealousy. Quent had surprised me, though. I had other physicians I adored and raved about— usually middle-aged men who were heavy or balding—and Quent had never considered quitting his physician to give them a try.

Hmmm. In hindsight, I think maybe Quent did ask what my new doctor looked like. That itself was unusual. He didn't ask what my overweight gynecologist looked like or my jovial dentist. Someone must have tipped him off about Dr. Matthews' boyish charms. When put on the spot to give my husband my opinion, I'd intentionally not lied but I'd downplayed it and said that the doc was cute and sorta reminded me of my little brother. Which, I swear, is true because they're about the same age and talk in similar youthful jargon. It's just that Dr. Matthews was far younger at the time than his predecessors, by at least twenty years.

I'd been a steady believer in the previous two physicians at the clinic, both of whom had left suddenly after about five years of practicing there. Hmmm, I hope that isn't a precursor of Dr. Matthews' departure in another year.

When I'd started limping after a workout at the gym at work, my boss at that time had urged me to see my family doctor about what had turned out to be a bad case of tendonitis. Nervous, I called Dr. Jordan's office and was told he'd just left medicine, but they had a brand new doc coming in, fresh out of med school. Before I could protest, the receptionist explained that he was very good, very friendly, the top of his class, and oh, yes, very cute. I laughed and told her she'd had me at "top of his class."

The moment he walked into my exam room and shook my hand four years ago, I knew I'd known him in a past life. I had that sense of…recognition…that I get with people I've known before, and I had it with him instantly. Probably the strongest I've ever had in my life, and that includes with Jan, Belinda, and my own children.

I knew there had been a healer in a particular past life in the sixth century and that the healer had helped my lover and me escape a group of warlords who wanted to kill us. He'd been very important to me. Perhaps Dr. Matthews was that healer, reborn. In any case, I sensed a connection but tamped it down. I wasn't new to Wicca then, but I was still shy about expressing my opinions to strangers.

And then the most incredible thing happened, something I still really don't understand but it sent shockwaves through me. He pulled up a stool and sat at my feet like a supplicant before the Goddess as he wrote down my medical history.

I find myself grinning at the memory. The door opens and catches me trying to stifle a smile as my gaze meets with Dr. Matthews'. The man has pretty eyes, a sort of blue-gray, and if it weren't so trite, I'd swear they twinkle. He always seems happy to see me, and today is no exception.

"Hello, hello, hello, Ms. Hartford!" He breezes into the room with his usual flourish, stethoscope draped around his neck. His legs seem to arrive ahead of him, like that old caricature of the Keep On Truckin' guy from the '70's. His arms are a little too long, enough so that he's already ditched the lab coat and unbuttoned his sleeves. They hang open at his wrists, obviously too short for his physique. He flips through my chart and rearranges a couple of pages as he stands with his back to me and makes a few notes.

"I was just thinking about you yesterday," he tells me without turning around.

"Really? Why?"

I can't imagine why he would have me on his mind. Judging by his tan, I would guess that he spent the day on a boat in the Gulf of Mexico with his gorgeous blonde and leggy wife. As for me, I've let the gray show through in my ponytailed hair, I'm a good thirty pounds heavier than my ideal weight, and I feel frumpy in my knee-length pink sweats and eye-watering yellow "World's Greatest Mom" T-shirt. My only salvation today is that I shaved my legs this morning, which I considered only polite if I was going make anyone look that closely at my swollen, tree-trunk knees today.

His face is animated. He opens his mouth before he speaks as if hoping the right words will magically pour out. "I read a story on the Internet about this Wiccan High Priestess up in New England. She's being persecuted for her beliefs, and I remembered that you're Wiccan, too."

He jots something on my chart. I have no idea what—he hasn't looked at my legs yet. He's still turned away from me, but not fully.

"And here you are, in the Bible Belt, which is so much more dangerous for you, and you're open about your beliefs and who you are. I think that is sooooo cool. I mean, you live in the middle of suburbia and you're a witch! A practicing witch! And nobody really knows. I mean, you wear a pentagram around your neck and people still don't know who you are. You just do your own thing and live what you believe in. You don't know how much I admire that."

I feel myself blush. I'm not used to praise. I'm even less used to someone understanding me or seeing me the way I want to be.

He glances up, a little shy when he meets my eyes. "You amaze me, Ms. Hartford."

If the purpose of his confession was to make me feel special, he's done it yet again. He probably tells every patient he was thinking of them yesterday. Or maybe not, come to think of it. That would be disingenuous, and he seems too honest to play those games.

In spite of his cheerfulness, there's something about Dr. Matthews that's sad today. I can't quite put my finger on it, but I can almost feel it in him. He's as friendly and as outgoing as he's ever been, but there's a bittersweetness in his voice. Maybe he's just having a bad day. Or maybe things didn't go so well with that last patient, the one he did a "procedure" on. He's always seemed the sensitive type, so if he had bad news to give a patient, I'm betting he can't detach himself from it that easily and be all smiles for the patient behind Door Number Two.

I expect him to ask me about Quent. Quent's his patient, too, and Dr. Matthews always asks. Whenever Quent's in for a visit, Dr. Matthews always asks after me, too. That's just the way the doc is. He never has trouble remembering our names or medical history or the stories we've told him about our families or jobs. He seems to have a killer memory just like I do, the kind of memory that can be more of a curse than a blessing. I bet his Mercury is in Aquarius, too, like mine and like my friend Belinda's. He has that hot mind that jumps all over, running on four-tracks at one time. Maybe a little ADHD, like I am, though his hyperactivity seems stronger than mine and he doesn't seem to have a problem paying attention while I'm in his office. His focus is solely on me.

"So how's Quent?" he asks, right on cue. Before I can answer or mention the divorce proceedings, he adds, "Tell him I expect to see him in here for that physical. No more canceling appointments because the two of you are off on some *looooooove* cruise." He makes a joke of the word and winks at me.

Cruise? My mind's a jumble. He must be confusing Quent with someone else. The doc does seem a little out of it today. "Quent cancelled an appointment?"

Dr. Matthews jerks his head up, eyes widening with that deer-in-headlights look. Like he's said too much. Like I was supposed to have known something. Like he thought I knew. But I didn't. And now he knows that I didn't know. And he knows I know something I'm not supposed to know. That Quent lied to me about his last doctor's appointment. He's been lying about other things, too.

"Yeah, uh…uh…." Dr. Matthews' boyishness comes out. He sounds like a little boy who's been caught chewing a double mouthful of bubble gum in church and doesn't know whether to swallow the gum or hide it in his hand. "Just, uh, tell Quent I asked about him, okay? Now, uh—" His hand shakes as he sets my medical chart on a desk full of months-old magazines. I've never seen him so unnerved. "Let's look at these knees, shall we, Ms. Hartford?" He emphasizes the *Ms.* He knows I'm married and that I kept my maiden name, which he's told me before that he thinks that's "so tres cool."

He breezes across the room to the sink and washes his hands quickly and efficiently, rubbing at the spot where he usually wears his wedding band. He's not wearing it today, but I assume it's a germ risk and it's safer if he doesn't. I've stopped wearing my wedding band, just these last couple of weeks, and I feel naked without it. Obviously, he does, too, even for a few minutes.

Gingerly, he raises the knee-length hems of my sweatpants and examines my knees. He touches my knee caps carefully, tenderly. "Oh, yeah, that's a lot of swelling, a lot of swelling."

I explain to him the situation with my knees and work and how much they hurt. He asks if the pain interferes with my quality of life and I confess without averting my eyes, that I'm having trouble getting up and down from the toilet. I'm surprised at my own candor, even with a doctor, but he doesn't blink. It's like whatever I say is okay.

I tell him about my old fencing injury and how long it's been and then we get sidetracked, talking about sabers and foils and epees and why a lightweight foil might be preferable to a broadsword in a fight to the death because you could land a killing blow more quickly with the lighter weapon. Then somehow, we're talking about the likelihood of female gladiators—or not—and how humanity has fared better under matriarchies and why he's a staunch supporter of female supremacy and the idea of a Goddess and a huge fan of what he calls "female-led marriage." And from there we're talking about chimpanzees and how similar they are to humans physically and socially and how female chimps dominate and the male chimps let them and still get all the sex they could ever want. And then he launches into how he's always wanted to go to the jungles of Central America on as humanitarian mission with Rick, his friend from Med School.

    I'm the one who reminds him of my knees. I tell him I have five weeks of vacation coming up soon and hopefully I'll be able to stay off my knees then and let them heal but I can't take time off for a few more weeks because of my hectic work schedule. Before that, I have a spiritual retreat to attend—which launches more questions from him on the type of retreat, who'll be there, how often we gather, if I have a local group yet. He has some female friends who might be interested in studying with me, he says. Then, getting back to my knee problem, he agrees that the time off will be a good idea and recommends ice, rest, elevation…and physical therapy for the next four to six weeks.

    The last thing he does is squat in front of me and take off my shoes. They're sandals that slip off without unbuckling and his touch is very gentle but a little awkward, almost like a little boy. It's endearing in a way. He catches his lower lip in his teeth as he presses against my arches and ankles. He explains to me that sometimes fallen arches can cause problems at the knees, which I myself have read. One's foundation, once crumbling, can affect your whole structure. He talks about pain meds, anti-inflammatory drugs, shoe heels, and the need to pamper myself. I answer his questions, but he's a little distracted.

"Hey, you're Wiccan, right?" He looks up at me from where he crouches in front of me. He already knows the answer. He's scattered. He's already forgotten our conversation from a few minutes ago or either his mind has jumped to another track. Mentally, he bounces and it keeps me on my toes. "I mean, I know you're Wiccan, but I have a question."

I touch the triskele pendant on my amethyst and ruby zoisite necklace as he examines my feet. For the last several visits to his office, my spirit guides have insisted I wear my pagan and Goddess jewelry openly, and every time, he's commented on it positively. There's something familiar about him, about this, the way he lifts his chin to look up at me from below. It's...disturbingly intense. I wonder if he was a student of mine in a past life.

"You know, Ms. Hartford, some people believe there's a connection between mind, body, and spirit. You know, a metaphysical connection? So like there might be a metaphysical cause that has a physical manifestation?"

I grin and nod. "Yeah, like I've been down on my knees too much in the past year."

"I know exactly how you feel." He smiles meaningfully and says nothing else about it. Instead, he replaces my sandals and gives each arch a little pat. "You've got great arches, you know? No problem there. Just in your knees. I'm gonna order some X-rays as a precaution, but I don't expect to find anything bad. Just a little knee strain and maybe a touch of arth—uh...wear and tear from all that lunging and parrying you did while winning fencing tourneys. But you're gonna have to lay off the heels. You're a flats girl from now on!" He grins, more to himself than to me.

While the doctor jots down a prescription for physical therapy and X-rays, a crow lights on the window ledge outside, taps on the glass with his beak, and peers in as if he can see us through the panes. A giggle tickles my throat and I'm surprised by it. I'm still not used to the sound of my own laughter. After the past few years, it sounds foreign to my ears.

The doctor looks over his shoulder at the crow and shoos at him with one hand. By coincidence, the crow flies away. "Sorry about that," he apologizes.

"No, it's okay. I *like* crows."

This time, he's the one who laughs. The sound comes out rich and warm. "You're unique, you know? I've never met anyone like you. So do crows mean something? You know, in Wicca?"

"Yes, they do—usually they're a symbol of destiny or a crow can be a messenger or an observer between the worlds—but they mean something very special to me."

He hands me the two prescriptions. "I didn't mean to pry. I mean, if it's private or—"

"No, no, it's not private at all. Okay, well, yes, it sorta is, but I don't mind sharing it with you. I'm dedicated to a particular Goddess. You've probably never heard of Her. The Morrigan. She's really sort of a Death Goddess but you don't necessarily have to look at Death in a physical sense. It can also be the death of an old way of life, which implies a new beginning, too. So, let's just say She's about transformation and change."

The deepening frown on his face relaxes a little with that last thought. "A Death Goddess?" he asks. "You're into the dark stuff?"

"Yeah, She *is* a Dark Goddess and I *do* practice Dark Magick, but *Dark* isn't *evil*, you know?"

He raises one eyebrow. Skepticism is written all over his face.

"The Morrigan, to me, is more about protection, defense. A warrior. She was the One who decided who would die in battle and who would live. She's the Dark Mother, the One who's always there for you in the darkest of times and cradles you when you can go no lower." I wince and he does, too, at the same time. The Dark Mother had held me through the worst of the nights after I'd confronted Quent about his extracurricular activities. "She's—"

He smiles. "Okay, I get it." He sinks his hands into his pockets and again poses himself as a little boy getting a lecture from his mother. "So why'd you pick a Dark Goddess? You know, instead of like—I don't know—Aphrodite or something?"

"I didn't pick Her. She picked me."

He nods and says nothing but takes it all in.

"The crows," I continue, rubbing my achy knees, "are to me like surrogate ravens, since they're cousins of the raven, you know? We don't have ravens around here."

"No, but we have plenty of crows! Especially in the past few days. They've been everywhere. Hardly seen any around here before. Are they migrating?"

"They seem to be staying put." Right over his building and the adjacent shopping center. As aware as I am of birds, I've noticed more red-tailed hawks and bluebirds in the past two seasons, but crows? Not here. Not until last week.

Something's going on. The Goddess is trying to tell me something.

"When I went through my Initiation," I explain, "I was blindfolded." His brow knits up again and I quickly add, "No big deal."

Though it *is* a big deal. There are things I'm oathbound not to reveal outside Dragon Hart, but Donna's told me I have the freedom to say certain things, more than most covens allow, but as my High Priestess, she's granted permission for me to talk. I've just never talked about these things before or had anyone I wanted to tell.

"The blindfold," I continue, "is really more symbolic than anything else. Having been in the dark all my life, et cetera, et cetera. Mystery. Trust."

"I see."

"Anyway, I was blindfolded, and during my Initiation, this yellow butterfly came down and lit on my head. All the Elders and Third Degrees who were there took it as a good omen. Butterflies represent metamorphosis, transformation. And then before we could go on with the ritual, this bird started cawing, interrupting the ritual and demanding to be heard, like he was approving it or something. My friend Leo's partner—Tyler—was part of the ceremony and he said later that it was a raven. Everyone had been amazed. They thought it meant something extra special. No one had ever seen that happen before."

Dr. Matthews leans against a work table and nods expectantly, waiting for more.

"I don't know if it was a raven or not. That was in Maryland and I don't know the birds up there. I was blindfolded and didn't see him. And I was a little busy with the ritual. But the raven is associated with The Morrigan. With my Goddess."

The doctor keeps nodding. "And the crows are like diminutive ravens, right? Because technically they're from the same family."

"I saw the same thing at my Second Degree Elevation—"

"Second...?" He looks confused. I seem to have a knack for frustrating him today.

"Yes. I'm in a formal training program. I went through a Dedication ceremony and a year later, I was Initiated. That was my First Degree in Dragon Hart Wicca, the year I learned more about my gifts and the Goddess. Then the next year—though it's often longer than a year—was my Second Degree ritual, the one where I became a High Priestess in my tradition or, um, like a denomination. During my Second Degree, I worked mainly with God energy and that's when my life turned upside down. It's been a phase of clearing out the problems in my life that I've failed to address in the past."

Like the abuse in my marriage. Like my codependency. Like letting my dreams die.

"And now, in two days, I go to my Third Degree Elevation, which is when I mesh the energies of God and Goddess and, according to the High Priestess who trained me, I begin to receive the gifts that are to come so that I can better serve Deity."

"Really." He rocks back on his heels. "So this is about over for you, right?"

"No. Actually, I think it's just beginning. That's what I'm told, anyway. I've heard that after this next Elevation, life will be a series of Second and Third Degree moments, all kinds of little trials still to get through to further me on my spiritual path."

"Wow," he says. "That's cool. So the crows outside the clinic, all these crows are sent by your Goddess?"

"Something like that."

"Wh-why my clinic?"

I shrug. "I think it has something to do with my knees. I'm ready to be transformed into someone who can stand on her own two feet without being in pain."

He and I both laugh. Gods, it feels good to laugh. I can't remember the last time I laughed with a—

"About Quent," I say, suddenly serious. "That cruise you mentioned that he went on…."

Dr. Matthews glances at an imaginary watch on his wrist. "Oh! I'm running an hour late! I've got several more patients today but it was…it was *groovy* seeing you again. You have a great day!"

He touches my shoulder in his usual friendly departure style, and the energy tingles deep into my flesh. Long after he's gone, I still feel it all the way to the bone.

I can't help the feeling that this man is either going to be my next student or he's going to be my next teacher.

5

Wednesday - Moon in Cancer, Waning Crescent

They say you can learn a lot about a person from his friends because he'll see in his friends the things that he admires: the things he either sees in himself or wants to see in himself. I guess you could say you could learn a lot about me just by looking at my friend Janice.

I ring the bell to the front door and wait. Somewhere in the distance, a dog yaps, and I know Jan's on her way through the house from her home office overlooking the lush gardens. A minute later, she opens the door, I step inside and, before she can close it, she gives me a big, warm hug. She's my best friend and my surrogate mother.

"Lauren!" She calls me by my mundane name, which is the only way she's ever known me. She can never remember my magickal name, but she knew me before I found the Goddess.

She ushers me inside with the dog between us, an aging German shepherd that weighs as much as I did when I first married. I've never seen anything remotely dangerous about this animal, in spite of her size, unless you count the bruises from her tail hitting your hipbone when she's wagging and happy to see you.

Most people, on seeing Jan and me for the first or even the fifth time, would never think we have anything in common. I'm a soon-to-be single mom in my early forties, but most people think I'm closer to 35 and even younger acquaintances refer to me as "Kiddo." My politics are fiscally conservative but liberal in regard to personal freedoms, and I'm a little outlandish in my thought patterns when people get to know me...which isn't right away. They see me fresh from the office, decked out in a suit, likely black or navy with matching pumps and maybe even pearls. Shy, quiet, reserved.

Jan, on the other hand, is anything but! She's in her early sixties, a burgundy-haired grandmother who refers to herself as "Grand" rather than Granny, and a full-time artist of some note, best known for her portraits of angels and a healthy poster-art business. Most people over twelve would recognize her work, even if they don't know her name. My kids' friends have posters of her art in their bedrooms and refer to the artist as "The Angel Lady." Her laugh ranges from a devilish snicker to a hardy guffaw. She is loving, maternal, a bit of a prude at times, overly conservative in her politics, and extremely moral. She's as good as her word, and anyone who isn't doesn't stay in her good graces for long.

She calls herself a "First Century" Christian who loves Jesus and Mother Mary, but her philosophy in the past few years has been more Wiccan than she realizes. She's a psychic, an empath, and she plays with crystals and candles as much as I do. I suspect she's caught my habit of having an altar in every room even though her altars are more likely to have Bibles and statues of the Archangel Michael, and only one of my altars is dedicated to Michael. Others have referred to her as a New Age Christian, but I know her for what she really is, what she could never call herself, if there is such a thing: a Christian Witch.

I slide into a wooden chair at the kitchen table, a patchouli-scented pillar candle burning in the handmade pottery dish between us. I set my oversized purse on the table next to me.

Today, Jan's wearing a combination of fire-engine red and violet purple—both ends of the chakra spectrum—and her cheeks are rosy. I assume it's been a good day and maybe she got another angel painted or signed a deal with a catalog company.

But no. She's taking a break and watching a movie on the kitchen TV. The rosy cheeks are the result of a heart-tugger that speaks to her. I recognize the movie as it ends and the credits roll. Diane Keaton and Jack Nicholson in *Something's Got to Give*.

"The older man's a better choice for her." Jan sniffs, referring to Keaton's love-hate interest in the movie.

"Ha!" I sip the glass of sweet tea she's put on the table in front me. "He's an old codger. She's too young and vibrant for him, even if she *is* pushing sixty. If I'd been her, I would've chosen the hot young doctor that Keanu Reeves plays."

Jan picks up the remote and clicks off the TV. "That's because you have more in common with a hot young doctor than you do with an older man."

I shrug. Either that or I still have an appreciation for Keanu Reeves onscreen. I've had a soft spot for him ever since *Bill and Ted's Excellent Adventure*. I squirm in my chair. "Keaton's character isn't the only one who's older than he is. I'm older, too."

"Doesn't matter. You need a younger man. Men your age can't keep up with you."

I blush. Jan knows why.

"Not just physically," she adds quickly before a somber mood can overtake me. "Mentally, too. Most men in their forties *think* old. You're not ready for that. Remember what your friend Leo told you about The Treat. I think you're going to be meeting him very soon. He feels so close! You've got someone wonderful coming into your life and I'll bet he doesn't think like a Grandpa or spend his time trying to figure out how to make himself feel young by fucking nineteen-year-olds."

That's my Jan. Blunt. She's generally soft-spoken and rarely crass, unless she's referring to my husband. Something about him always brings profanity to her lips.

"I'm not ready for any man right now, thank you. I just want to be by myself for a while."

"Hmmm. Speaking of old codgers, how is His Majesty?" She rises and walks to the door to light a cigarette. She blows the smoke out the door and turns to me to talk between puffs. She's been trying to quit ever since before Sonnet learned to crawl. For as strong as she is, it's the one thing she's never been able to kick.

"He's been out of the house for a week. He calls the girls every night and poor-mouths about having to leave and how broke and pathetic he is."

"Did you ever find out how much money he's hidden from you? I'm thinking it's close to a cool million."

I shake my head. "I don't think I'm meant to know. The investigator said that with Quent's job in the financial industry, he'd be able to hide all kinds of stuff and no one would ever be able to see it, let alone get to it. I just want to make sure he doesn't pull the religion card and try to take my girls from me."

"If he does, you've got all kinds of things you could expose on him."

I agree, but I don't see myself doing that. Not unless I'm backed into a corner. There are other things that happened with him, really scary things, but I've never told Jan. I never will. I'll never tell anyone. Not even my doctor.

"He did finally go back to the doctor," I say after a few seconds of silence. "I've been begging him to since February and he kept refusing. But after I filed the divorce papers, he agreed. He tried to make it to an appointment in June but a business trip got in the way. Finally got an appointment with Dr. Matthews a couple of weeks ago. At least that's what he told me. The tests results aren't in yet."

"Well, let's hope it's not AIDS. You really have no idea where that prick has been." Then she smirks. "Or his penis."

"Jan, I don't think he saw Dr. Matthews. Or any doctor. I think he lied about it."

"Son...of...a bitch. Yeah. Yeah, he's lied about it. I can see that. He asked you to make the appointment for him and then he called and cancelled it because of a business trip he had to make." She gazes out the window at the wilted impatiens in the August sunshine. She's perfectly still for just a moment, then makes a face and nods her head. "Business trip, my ass! Who's the blonde woman he's with? They're on a cruise. Alaska? No business trip about it unless you count monkey business." She shakes her head, shakes away the vision, then tamps out the cigarette and returns to her chair. "How are you set for money right now? You need to borrow some?"

I catch my bottom lip between my teeth and try to figure out how to tell her I'm in trouble. "No. No, I'm fine. He hasn't paid any child support yet, he didn't pay some big bills over the summer, and my bank account's frozen...but I'll manage."

"You're sure?" Jan sounds skeptical. I'm lying to a psychic, but she allows it to pass and lets me keep my dignity as I nod.

"What I'm mostly worried about is that he'll hold it against me if I leave the girls with him for two extra days while I go to my Elevation ceremony in Maryland tomorrow."

"Tomorrow? Did I lose track of time? We're going to have two hurricanes coming toward us tomorrow. Did you know that?"

I expel a long breath. "Yeah. But I have to get there. Lady Dragon insists on being at all Third Degree Elevations. So if I don't go, I don't get my Third. I've worked too hard for this. But at the same time, I don't want Quent telling the judge I'm off with my cult and neglecting my kids."

Jan digs under some newspapers and through the day's mail and hauls out a brown envelope similar to the one in my purse. "By the way, this came for you yesterday."

It's my Third Degree exam, graded and annotated. I know it before I touch the package. I slip it under my purse without opening the envelope. "Sorry about it coming here. Donna told Lady Dragon you were my friend and that maybe any mail from her should go to you until Quent moved out."

"No problem. And don't worry about Quent telling the judge you're out of town for two whole days. How often has he been gone—or said he was gone—and left you all alone with the girls? At least three times this summer that I know of."

"I know that's a logical argument, Jan, but when you're talking about pagan parents fighting to keep custody here in the Bible Belt, you just never know. And he keeps bringing up my 'cult' activity."

"But it's not a cult. It's a—" Jan stops. "What's wrong?"

Sucking in a deep breath, I reach into my oversized purse for the package from the anonymous sender. "I'm not so sure that Dragon Hart isn't a cult."

"What?" The word comes out so loud that her dog startles and wakes from her spot on the floor near the wall. Jan lowers her voice. "Lauren Hartford, I know you. You would never get involved with a cult."

"True. I didn't. But some things have happened over the past year. Things I just now found out about. It wasn't a cult but Lady Dragon's done some things that… well, it's becoming a cult—fast."

Jan gets up and paces. She sits. Then she gets up again. "I don't believe this," she says from across the room. "I have heard nothing but good about this group. And you've learned so much. What the hell is going on?"

I open the top flap of the package. I'm nervous. I shouldn't be sharing this information with anyone outside the Grand Coven, but I can't really share it with anyone inside the Grand Coven either. Donna's already warned me not to. It could get me kicked out before I get my Third. I shouldn't question anything openly before my Elevation. Donna doesn't want her name associated with this anonymous package either. None of the Elders do. Not yet. Maybe not ever. I don't want to tick off Lady Dragon, they've said.

I drop the photocopied checklist on top of the package. "I've spent five days now going through this package, doing research online, trying to see what my head tells me, trying to see what my gut tells me, and Jan, I swear, I just don't know. This checklist on top? There was a note in the package, said to fill out the checklist before I read the package. And then to fill it out again afterward." I pull another checklist from the bottom of the stack. "To fill out a second copy after I'd read the papers."

Jan shifts her shoulders. "What is it?"

"The checklist is one created by Issac Bonewits. Same one I found at his website." For a second, I forget she isn't pagan. And that she doesn't know the name. "Bonewits is a well-known occultist. Modern-day pagans really owe him a lot for what he brought to us. He wrote a book called *Real Magic* back in the early '70s. And in it, he included a checklist to help the reader discern whether his or her group is actually a cult. It's called the 'Advanced

Bonewits' Cult Danger Evaluation Frame.' Basically, to see if the group dynamics are healthy. A total of eighteen factors, if I remember correctly, each with a scale of 1 to 10. Over the years, he's revised the checklist—it's all over the Internet—but it's still one of the best tools for looking at any religious organization to see if there's cult activity present."

Jan looks concerned. "And is there?"

"I…I don't know. I knew—or thought I knew—before I filled out the checklist, before I knew what was in this package. I thought I knew that I hadn't joined a cult but a legitimate religious organization that would give me formal training and help me shed some of the issues I had that weren't good for me. So when I went through the checklist the first time, out of 180 possible points, I scored Dragon Hart as a 61. When I finished reading the package, I looked at the things that had happened in the past one to two years with Dragon Hart. Jan, I scored it at 140 points."

"The score doubled in one to two years?"

"Yeah, but that still doesn't necessarily make it a cult. It's suggested that it might be an unhealthy group if they score over 150."

"Still, doubling in one to two years? After how many years has this organization has been in existence?"

"Twenty. Yes, I know. This one has me alarmed. There are plenty of things on the checklist that don't apply, though. I mean, for example, there's not violence used to keep people from leaving the group. Lady Dragon doesn't lead an opulent lifestyle while her congregation is penniless. There's no forced sex or special favors or anything of that sort. People aren't told they can't talk to their families."

"All of what you normally consider to be cult activity."

"Right. But this isn't a cult according to the scores, and yet I don't know, Jan. There's something wrong. Just wrong here. I don't think it was like this always. I don't think it was like this a couple years ago. But something's happened in the past year, maybe two years. All after I came into the Grand Coven. Around the time my friend Belinda left."

"Have you talked to Belinda about it?"

I shake my head. "Haven't seen Belinda in a while. You know that bothers me, too. She and I were friends and did a lot of Goddess work together as solitaries. She's the one who brought me into Dragon Hart. And then just before my Initiation, she left and never said why. She wouldn't talk about it, you know. Said I was welcome to go with her and her group, but she'd leave it up to me. Leave it up to the Goddess. And she'd understand whatever decision I made. And I made a decision to stay. I know that kind of surprised her, and me, too. Even Lady Dragon. Everyone expected me to go with Belinda. But it didn't feel right. For some reason, I was supposed to stay with Dragon Hart."

"Following your heart is good. What does it tell you now?"

"Now I don't know. But at the first Grand Coven meeting after Belinda had left the group, I made the mistake of mentioning her name and a Pagan Pride Day project I was going to help her with. And everybody around me went dead silent. All of a sudden, three of the Elders—the Elders have always liked me, you know?—they jumped up and started making a commotion about something else. Totally changed the subject. They started talking loud enough that no one else could hear what I was saying. Later, Donna pulled me aside and explained that I couldn't talk about Belinda anywhere around the group or to anyone in the group, but that I really shouldn't see her or talk to her again since she was no longer in the group. Not just don't talk to her about group business but don't talk to her *at all.* And that I wasn't to tell anyone in Dragon Hart that I still had contact with her, especially not Lady Dragon."

"Why the hell not?" Jan pours herself a second glass of tea and tops mine off. "You and Belinda stayed friends after she left the group and you stayed. That says a lot for your friendship."

"I know, but the official party line was, Belinda had left the group so we didn't need to exert any more energy thinking about her or talking about the circumstances under which she left or worrying about her personal welfare."

"Wait a minute. Didn't she leave to start her own coven or church or whatever?"

"Yeah. She didn't leave with any animosity toward Lady Dragon or anyone there. She left to start a series of Earth-based churches across New York, Pennsylvania, New Jersey, and Connecticut. It was something she felt the Goddess pressing her to do and she didn't feel she could do it while she was a member of Dragon Hart. Yet, when she told Lady Dragon she felt led to leave, she was thrown out and cut off—immediately. I understand Lady Dragon not wanting to exert any more energy on someone who's not part of her group, but telling everyone else to avoid her? It didn't make sense, Jan."

"Yes, it does. It's called *shunning.*"

Shunning. I'd seen it in some of the small Baptist churches in my hometown. A pregnant teenager suddenly cast out by her fundamentalist parents, no one in her church speaking to her anymore for her Satan-begotten ways, whether they were the results of a youthful indiscretion, or rape, or incest. But other than in a few backwoods country churches, I didn't think shunning was still done.

I nod slowly. "One of the Elders suggested that not only should I not mention Belinda's name again, but it would be best if I didn't associate with her at all. I told her she was crazy. That Belinda was my friend and I cared about her and I always would. I didn't have any problems with Belinda or anything she'd done, and nobody was going to tell me who I could be friends with. The Elders said okay, but that I should remember that if Lady Dragon found out I was still friends with Belinda, she might take it personally and cut me out of the group, too."

"And then you'd be shunned as well?"

"I suppose. Nobody ever called it *shunning*."

"Of course not. They never do, do they? But," Jan says, "you knew that already and you didn't leave."

"True. It seemed like a discrepancy. I didn't see a pattern in it, but there were other things I thought were odd." I shrug. "I'll allow people to have their eccentricities. I certainly have enough myself. And I really don't expect people to be perfect, regardless of what Quent says."

Jan makes a face. "You didn't expect Quent to be perfect. You just expected him to be honest. So have the papers changed your mind?" Jan swats her hand on top of the papers alleging Dragon Hart is headed for Cult Land. Her expression changes. "These didn't come from anyone inside your coven. You know that, don't you?"

I didn't. How could anyone who isn't a member of Dragon Hart get that information? Hell, how could any ordinary *member* get that info?

"This person likes you," Jan says, absorbing the vibrations from the papers through her palm. "Not in a sexual way, though. This is someone who is affiliated with the group or maybe was a member in the past. He's sorta there but not like he used to be. Maybe this is more about a lack of emotional attachment than a physical attachment to the group. That's how he knows you, though. Through the group. And it is a *he*."

I really don't know Lady Dragon very well. I've spoken to her maybe three times in the past three years, and once was when she told me she was grateful that my allegiance had stayed with her instead of...leaving. She'd meant, leaving to go with Belinda but she'd never said Belinda's name. The other two times were basically a hello, and that was it. She wasn't at my Dedication ceremony—

Belinda did that. She wasn't at my Initiation or at my Second Degree Elevation. She'd never been part of my sacred life and she'd not passed any power to me. Not yet, anyway.

Jan stabs a finger at the checklist. "How about this one? Where it suggests that that leader of the cults sets himself or herself up as being infallible? God incarnated or a 'chosen one' or something?"

"Technically, we're all chosen ones in my belief system. The Goddess chose each of us. And technically, Lady Dragon isn't any more chosen than, say, I am. So I don't know, Jan. I've never personally witnessed her setting herself up as being above anyone else, although some of emails in this package do seem to imply that. But I have seen other people set her up that way. At all the rituals I've ever been to at Grand Coven meetings, there's some type of mandatory tribute to her. They take turns every year at the main meetings and rituals with different small covens within the Grand Coven performing the five annual rituals that are done at these meetings. In every ritual, without fail, someone hauls out a wicker chair or a bar stool or something and they make a big deal of calling Lady Dragon out of the crowd and having her come sit on her imaginary throne so they can thank her for everything she's done for all of us. It's…well, it's become a joke among the Elders. She doesn't enforce it. It's just something that people feel they need to do."

"What about this one?" Jan rubs her finger along a line of ink but I'm not really listening. I'm lost on the last question.

"Another thing I've noticed is that the last few times I've seen her, she had…bodyguards…sorta…around her. There were two Third Degree women and a Third Degree man, and several students who stayed within three feet of her, no matter what. Donna and Beverly tried to have a private conversation with her and absolutely had to run the bodyguards off to do it. The bodyguards didn't want her to be alone with anyone. I could see it with a stranger or even a newbie to the group, like me, but with Donna and Beverly? Two of her oldest friends? And the Elders? They've known each other for over twenty years. Donna and Beverly were the first two Elders, and the ones who talked Lady Dragon into expanding the sitting-on-the-living-room-floor lessons into a Grand Coven spanning half the states in the country and into Canada and Mexico. They had some great mission they were supposed to do. I don't know what it was, but Donna always referred to it as 'the mission.' She won't talk specifics, just that the mission given to Lady Dragon by the Goddess has not yet come to fruition. I know it's caused tension among the Elders and I know someone else planned to leave to try it, but they finally all agreed that it's really up to Lady Dragon. The mission was given specifically to her, not to them."

"Hmmm," Jan says. "Having a mission. That could be looked at as cult activity. You know, having a mission from God? Something that makes them infallible or un-usually important?"

"Maybe. But when I was a Southern Baptist Christian, we had a mission, too, and that was to convert all the heathens, so I don't necessarily see that as cult activity. I guess it would depend on the mission though, and since I don't know what it is...." I shrug.

"Taking money from church members," Jan says, tapping a line of print. "How about that one? Any evidence?"

"Not so much money as other things that equate to money and, more importantly, to power. I know she sells electronic files of books and spiritual lessons on eBay and from her website. She didn't write any of those books or lessons. She sells artwork from her site, too. She doesn't paint, but I've been told that one of her Third Degrees does. As her student's Third Degree challenge, Lady

Dragon had the student paint a series of posters that were later turned into prints, Tarot cards, greeting cards, T-shirts. She sells a lot of these as her own."

"What?" Jan, artist that she is, is immediately incensed. Before she begins to lecture me on copyright law and intellectual rights, I hold up my hand and continue.

"There's an email in here, or a copy of it, and the email politely asks why she's been selling the work as her own. There's an answer back that says the artist gave up rights to Lady Dragon as part of his training and the questioner shouldn't be concerned because the proceeds from the artwork is going to support the Dragon Hart charity."

"What charity is that?"

"I don't really know."

"Lady Dragon, perchance?"

"Like I said, I don't really know. Just 'charity.' That's what the email says."

"Do you know the artist?"

I nod. "He's still affiliated with the group though not very active. Leo's husband. Tyler."

Jan starts to say something, but I stop her. She keeps shaking her head.

"There have been allegations by the Elders," I continue, "that Lady Dragon has sold some of their own work over the years as her own, including material from their personal Book of Shadows."

"Book of...?" Jan blinks. "That's a magickal journal, right?"

"Yeah. And very personal. Spells and insights and things. You can show it to someone else if you want, but in general, it's kept very private. You might show your High Priestess or High Priest but usually no one else. Mariah's boyfriend complained that his Book of Shadows had been scanned into a computer file and copies of it sold for $20 a download. That's a big part of why the Elders are unhappy with Lady Dragon."

"Lauren! That's more than being unhappy with someone—that's unethical! And...and illegal."

I nod. "It's the opposite of what she teaches, too. People who don't know her consider her to be a fluffy bunny, always preaching dolphins, crystals, and moonbeams, but Jan, I swear, she's one of the darkest witches I've ever met and certainly one of the most unethical. It's not just stealing copyrights, but it's everything! There are bank statements in here that show where she's putting coven funds in her personal accounts."

"Mixing non-profit funds with personal?"

"That's just it, Jan. Dragon Hart is not non-profit religious foundation like everyone thinks. She never incorporated it. All this time, I thought it was a non-profit with a council and rotating board members and bylaws. You know, how it's supposed to be. But it isn't. She doesn't even have a separate bank account that coven funds are going into."

Jan whistles. "That's...fraud."

"And speaking of fraud, did I mention that she hasn't filed a tax return...*ever?*"

Jan's jaw drops. "What are the Elders doing about this? They've got to be doing something. Tell me they're doing something, right?"

"I wish I could, but...no. For some reason—and I can't understand why—they're all scared to death of her. But the latest email," I say as I pull a sheet of paper out of the stack, "was sent out last week before Donna told me she was leaving the group. As of Samhain this year...that's usually celebrated at Halloween on October 31st, but well, astrologically, it's around November 6th at 15 degrees into Scorpio...all Elder status is heretofore revoked. It doesn't matter if they've been an Elder for twenty years or twenty days. They're no longer Elders, and new Elders will be appointed by Lady Dragon at her convenience."

"What about the former Elders?"

"They'll be allowed to remain as Third Degrees but without any power or checks in the check-and-balance against Lady Dragon. Or they're free to go start their own organizations far, far away."

"So shut up or get out?"

"Yes. And most are getting out."

"But they're Elders," argues Jan. "She can't just kick them out on a whim."

"Sure, she can. She's the High Priestess of the Grand Coven and what she says goes. And the word of the High Priestess takes precedence, whether she's rational or not."

Jan chews on a piece of ice and crunches it down to nothing. "Lauren, if what you said about her not paying taxes is true…if she gets caught…it's not just her head on the platter."

"I know. It's mine, too. And everyone in Dragon Hart. And beyond. Every pagan in the country will be painted with the same brush by the media. I know, Jan. I know. Remember what I told you about the Healing Center and the Center of Light and how it felt like I was being given this—I hate to use the word—*mission* by the Goddess to start these centers around the country? Whatever you want to call it, I know there's something special that the Goddess wants me to do and I know that it can't be associated with Lady Dragon. At all."

Jan nods. "If she's the type of person you've been describing to me today, she'll take credit for whatever project you work on. Just like she's taken credit from artists and students and everyone around, and it'll become about her instead of about the service to your Goddess."

"And service to humanity. These Centers of Light…Jan, they're going to be important. It's something I really, really feel people are going to need. My heart just yearns to do it. Do you know what I mean?"

Jan smiles. "Sure do. Because I'm going to be do-ing it with you, too. Not as a pagan, but...I'm not quite sure how yet, but I'm going to be involved, too."

"I know."

"If Lady Dragon gets involved, she'll taint them. I can't let her do that, Lauren. She'll suck you dry. Like so many other people in your life, she'll take your fire. She'll drink your cup until there's nothing left. Like Quent. Like Scott. She'll do it, too."

I startle at the mention of Scott's name. I haven't thought much about him in years. My old flame. I don't want to think of him now either.

"There are other things about Lady Dragon that bother me," I tell Jan. "I've seen hints of it. The way she uses their energy. Uses them almost like batteries for her own rituals."

"That's not right. That's abuse."

"Exactly as alleged in these papers. In one place, she tells the Elders that they've been used up and don't have any energy anymore and that's why she needs new Elders. I've never heard of anything like this before. I was always taught by Donna and the Elders that you do things ethically, that you don't use people, that whatever you send out returns to you threefold. I don't understand how a spiritual leader who knows these things and teaches about karma could not practice what she preaches."

"Easy." Jan laughs. "Spiritual leaders do it all the time, sweetheart. That's why it's important to divorce yourself from them when they do. It's just as important for you to remember when you're a spiritual leader not to ever do that to anyone else. Look, I know you love your coven, but I think it's time for you to give them up and strike out on your own. Go with the Elders if you feel you must, but I think you're going to do best blazing new trails without them, too. But whatever you do, don't go it with Lady Dragon."

"But Jan—"

"Girl, there are two hurricanes coming this way. You think your plane's going to take off? I'm seeing that you're not supposed to go. You don't need this Third Degree Elevation. Maybe the hurricanes are a message that you're not supposed to go."

"No. No, it isn't." I'm arguing with a psychic, yes, but I know without a doubt. "I'm supposed to be there."

"Look, I wasn't going to tell you this, but I had this dream, and you know how I never remember my dreams."

I stifle a laugh. Jan has dreams all the time and never remembers that she remembers her dreams.

"Lauren, you know how I've asked God not to give me dreams or visions or messages unless I'm supposed to pass them on? I had this dream and I remember it, so I know I'm supposed to pass it on to you but you're not going to like it." She wrinkles her brow. "I dreamed you went to this ceremony in Maryland and there were all these people in black robes standing in a circle around you." She shudders.

I don't say anything. In her Christian background, robed figures in black? Not a good thing. For me, it's not a problem. I take Jan very seriously when she recounts her dream because very soon, I *will* be in a circle of the figures in black robes, just as she describes.

"They were chanting, Lauren. You were on the ground and there was some type of sacrifice being made. They were putting candles around your body. Incense. A rock. A cauldron of water. I think you were about to be sacrificed."

"That's not...."

"You're bleeding."

"Bleeding? Where?"

"I...I don't know. From inside. I don't see any cuts or wounds, though. Lauren, why would you be bleeding from the inside?"

I shrug it off, but uneasily. What is she interpreting as a human sacrifice? My group doesn't believe in that. Animal sacrifice, either.

"Jan, I'm going."

She stares at me, appalled for not taking her advice as I usually do. "Nothing I say will change your mind?"

"No. I'm going."

"What are you going to do? Are you going to leave the group or not?"

"I don't know. I honestly do not know."

But what scares me the most is why the Elders, some of the most powerful witches in the country, are so afraid of Lady Dragon.

6

Thursday - Moon in Cancer, Waning Crescent

My older daughter throws her arms around me and pretends her contact lens is causing the tears in her eyes. That or the mascara she's borrowed from me. She squeezes me and doesn't let go.

"I want to come, too." Rhiannon sniffs into my shoulder, leaving the strong scent of raspberry shampoo on my T-shirt.

She doesn't say, "Don't go." She understands how important this trip is to me. She wants to be there for me, too, and to see Donna and Leo and all "Mom's cool friends" from the year before. But she knows that this year, it's just not possible. It's her first year of high school, and school's already started here in the Bible Belt. She's afraid she'll never catch up if she misses the first week of school, which is what she'd miss if I drove up to Maryland like I did last year.

She knows, too, that I'm going to my Elevation with a heavy heart, that I haven't decided on whether I'll stay with Dragon Hart or leave. Donna says I have all week-end, but making up my mind is still my Third Degree challenge. I don't want to leave. I love the people of Dragon Hart. But it's our leader who confounds me.

"When will you be back?" Rhiannon asks, pulling away and swiping at her tears. She's 14, and she looks so grown up and so young all at the same time, especially in my black ankle boots. She's already bigger than I was when I married at 24. "Will you be home before Monday?" she presses. "Or will Sonnet and I have to spend another night with Daddy?"

"I'll be back Sunday night." It's Thursday morning now, about 6 a.m. "If I get to leave."

I say it jokingly, but I'm dead serious. The phone has already rung twice since 4 a.m. to let me know my flight has been delayed. At the moment, I'm booked on the 9 a.m. flight, which means I'll need to leave in another 30 minutes to make it to the airport on time.

Rhiannon pauses to look me in the eyes. She's only about two inches shorter than I am. "Aren't you afraid?"

"Of Lady Dragon? No." I laugh to prove it. I don't feel afraid of nearly so much now that Quent's moved out of the house. I feel lighter, freer. Life is good. Manless, yes, but that part doesn't matter, even if Leo does say I have a *Treat* coming into my life soon. "I'm not afraid of Lady Dragon."

"No, the storms."

Oh. The storms. Yes, that part worries me. Tropical Storm Bonnie is close to hurricane strength but doesn't look like it'll make the final notch. Charley is close behind, maybe two days later. The aircraft I'm supposed to be on has been delayed because it can't take off from the last place it landed and fly back to the Florida Panhandle. And once it gets here, it may not be able to take off. It seems Mother Nature is conspiring against me.

Or someone is.

"Please be safe, Mommy." Rhiannon pulls back and peers into my eyes, "If something were to happen to you...."

I know the rest without her saying it. If something were to happen to me, if I were to die in a plane crash, for example, what would happen to Rhiannon and her little sister? They'd have to live with their dad full-time, that's what.

"But have a good time," she adds. "Really, I wish I were going. You have a good time. You have a good time for me, too, okay? And maybe...."

"Maybe what?"

"I don't know. I was going to say maybe you'd meet a nice guy. Like The Treat. Maybe you'll meet him this weekend."

"No," Sonnet moans as she exits the bathroom and promptly wraps her arms around my waist. "No men."

Rhiannon sighs. "I kind of agree, Mommy. Sonnet and I have been talking and...and we think that once your divorce with Daddy is done, that maybe you shouldn't date. Not for a while."

Sonnet squashes her face against my chest. "Not ever."

"Look, girls." I kneel beside them and hug them both. "I have no intention of dating anyone, but at some point I probably will start dating again. You know, just to have some male companionship."

The girls exchange glances, and I know they've been talking a lot more than they're saying. Most likely on the nights when Rhiannon has crawled into bed with Sonnet, at Sonnet's invitation, and they've whispered for hours.

"You...you made some bad choices with Daddy," Rhiannon says at last. "And we're afraid that if you start dating, that it will mean someone new and that you'll fall in love with him and that he'll be just like Daddy. So we would rather you just not date."

Sonnet nods into my chest. "Not ever."

My eyes sting. Maybe they're right. I made such a bad choice with Quent. Or at least it became a bad choice over the years if it wasn't a bad choice in the beginning. And I never saw it, never knew it. How will I ever know if a new man is good for me or not? What will keep me from making the exact same mistake all over again? Even if there really is a *Treat* out there, I'm not sure I can trust myself where men are concerned. Not anymore.

I stroke Sonnet's long brown hair. It breaks my heart the way she's changed in the past year. Until a year ago, she'd been a happy child, with occasional bouts of empathy that I had not understood at the time. Like the time Quent locked me out of the bedroom because I'd worn a dress he didn't like. And Sonnet had felt my anxiety in her gut, and had hidden in bed, trembling and crying and not understanding.

She's gained twenty pounds in the past year, all on her tiny frame. All without any other explanation other than a metaphysical one—protective padding. She's deliberately made herself as unattractive as possible in the past year. The baggy clothes she wears, the way she styles her hair, insisting on wearing the ugliest glasses, all in an effort to make sure no man could find her interesting. Even though she's only eleven years old.

I told her just this past weekend that she couldn't see a PG-13 movie with me, and I felt like such a hypocrite. After all, she's seen worse than any PG-13's suggested innuendos and failed sex scenes. She's seen it all. She's seen things I didn't even know existed until I was in my thirties. And I don't think I'll ever forgive Quent for it, and I don't think she will either.

Last year, when I came back from the Dragon Hart Grand Coven meeting, while Rhiannon and I had spent ten days on the road and camping, bonding, getting to know each other and understand each other beyond all superficial surfaces, the baby I had left back home with her father had lost her innocence. Exactly as Leo had said, Quent was up to his old tricks again. Though he'd sworn off the pornography and the escort services to save our marriage and to prove that he could quit his porn addiction cold turkey, he never had. He never slowed up at all.

He had, as Leo had said, hidden it better. But while I was gone, he didn't bother to hide anything. He didn't have to worry about erasing the cookies from the computer or making any type of changes at all until I returned, and it was during that time that he allowed Sonnet to play on his computer, unsupervised.

She had been slender, cute, and full of sparkles at the time, and all she wanted was to find a website that had ribbons and bows she could weave into a long braid. Instead she clicked on a site in his browser history, one that seemed to be about girls. His favorite hardcore porn site had appeared on the screen in front of her in full color, in full detail.

Fisting, double penetration, anal sex, facials, women in bondage and women in pain, women being raped. All of it right there in front of her. Women with farm animals.

She had panicked and tried to click out of the website, but for every click she made, three more pop-ups appeared on the screen. The more frantically she tried to make them all stop, the more insistent they were, the more persistent. They proliferated in front of her.

Pop-up screens with videos. Full audios of women moaning, some in pleasure and some screaming for mercy.

When I returned from my trip and found what was in the Internet history and confronted Quent about it, the fucker played the innocent.

"Oh, that's not mine," he'd sworn, "It must have been Sonnet. She must have been the one who brought that filth into this house. Unless it was you. It sure wasn't me."

Bastard. Goddamned Bastard. To do that to my little girl! For months afterward, she'd not been able to even look up at a man. She saw a man on the street, she looked away. All men became evil to her, particularly her dad. The same went for her male teachers. Her grades had plummeted overnight in every class taught by a man.

She'd hugged me in the dark of night in the protective realm of her bed behind a locked bedroom door. And she had told me, "It's body parts, Mommy; just body parts."

And I had looked at her and wondered, how will she ever think of sex as an act of love with everything she's seen? She'd been damned near catatonic for months after that.

And yes, Quent can blame the divorce for everything going on inside her right now, but she's already told me she wants nothing to do with men when she grows up. That she's decided she's going to be a lesbian. I've had her in and out of private counseling all year to talk through what she's seen. But what I could kick myself for more than anything else is that I actually stayed with her father for another six months after he blamed her for his indiscretions.

Fucking bastard.

I send both girls off to the school bus. What have I done? What have I done by staying married to their father? I should have left him years ago.

But if I had, they might remember the man he was, the man who used to play with them when they were little. Instead of as the man he is now. And they would never have understood my leaving him.

Then again, if it weren't for the Dragon Hart Grand Coven, I never would have had the courage to find myself again and reclaim my life. I can't change what happened in the past, but I can change the future. Our future. Theirs, too.

The phone rings and I know before I pick up that it's the airline calling again to let me know my flight has been delayed. I'm right. My flight is now scheduled to take off at eleven o'clock and I'm to report to the airport at nine.

I'm alone in the house, my bags are packed, and I'm just waiting. Every now and then I turn on The Weather Channel and see that Bonnie, the tropical storm—or is it a hurricane already?—is closing in faster. If my plane doesn't hurry up and make it to the airport, I may not be going to Maryland today after all. If I miss the Grand Coven meeting, I'll have to wait maybe even another year for this chance to get my Third Degree.

I don't want to stay a Second Degree any longer. It's been terrible. It's been harsh. I've made the changes. I'm ready. I want my Third Degree, and I want it badly. But the meteorologist on TV points to twin storms coming. And right now I just don't see this Elevation ritual happening for me this weekend.

Maybe I should do a ritual to calm myself down. Rituals are good for many things, not just raising energy, but calming it, too. Maybe just a few quiet moments.

I step out into the backyard, out into what was once my sanctuary, but I've let it grow up and become overgrown with weeds over these last few years. I had things on my mind other than gardening.

What I really want is a sign. I love signs. I live by signs.

"Oh, Goddess, give me a sign that everything will be all right."

Everything in the backyard is quiet, eerily so. There's a surreal feel to this morning. Maybe it's the anticipation over my Third Degree. There's a funny blend of blue sky and clouds that are already swirling, and the tall pines have that swizzle-stick effect that they get during the widdershins circles of hurricanes. There's a smell of salty water in the wind.

I circle the fire pit I built last year. The one where the girls and I sit at least once a month and roast marshmallows and hotdogs and eat s'mores and look at the stars. On full moon nights and dark moon nights, my little campfire doubles as a bonfire. The wood inside the iron bowl still smolders, just enough that wisps of smoke occasionally escape into the sky.

I fling open my arms to the North, close my eyes, and lift my cheeks to the early morning sun in the East. I take a deep cleansing breath, then let it out slowly.

"Oh, Goddess, I don't know if I'm going to make it to Maryland or not today. It doesn't look that way. I'm worried. I'm really worried. I don't know what to do. I could back out, use the hurricane as an excuse and just not go to the Elevation. I'm so close to doing that right now. That would get me out of making this decision, or at least making it this weekend. But it doesn't solve my problems. I'm turning it over to You, Great Mother, my Goddess, and if I'm supposed to be there this weekend, if I'm supposed to get my Third Degree Elevation, then I'm putting it in Your hands to make it happen. You make it happen and I'll be there. You open the door for me to be there, and I'll willingly go."

I open my eyes to the sounds of crows flying overhead. Two of them. *One crow, sorrow. Two crows, mirth.* Then two more join them. *Three crows, a wedding. Four crows, birth.* A sudden tranquility pumps through my veins. Everything's going to be all right. It's all going to be okay. Four crows, the sign of rebirth, of starting over, a sign from the Goddess. Everything will be all right.

I'm hungry and I have no food in the house. I have a plane to board, but the plane's late and I have time on my hands now. I decided to go to the fast-food restaurant beside Dr. Matthews' clinic and get a breakfast biscuit and a cup of caffeine.

Ten minutes later, I sit smiling in a booth facing the eastern window of the restaurant. I'm happy, but I can't really explain why. I have this sense of calmness of know-ing everything will be all right. Before I can take the first bite of my breakfast biscuit, my cell phone rings.

"Have you seen The Weather Channel?" Jan de-mands before I get "Hello?" out of my mouth. "I think you better cancel this trip. I have a bad feeling about it. This Lady Dragon of yours, she's gonna be trouble. I think these hurricanes are just a way of making sure you don't go. And don't forget about my dream."

"I'm going, Jan." I'm surprised at the calmness of my own voice. "I'm supposed to be there."

"I don't know about that, sweetie. I know you want to go, but I just have a really bad feeling that something God-awful is going to happen while you're there."

"Something's going to happen, I agree, but I don't know what. All I know is that I'm supposed to be there."

Jan sighs loudly. "Okay, well, I'll light a candle for you, and I'm going to be praying for you to be protected. The Archangel Michael will be watching over you, protect-ing you, and a couple of saints will be, too."

I laugh. "Okay, Jan. I'll probably need them all."

"I'm serious, Lauren. I have a gut feeling that you're not going to be there for long. Do you want to know what I'm seeing?"

I hesitate. Most of the time, Jan's visions are right, but sometimes if she's too emotionally close to a subject, her sight becomes tainted. It becomes more of a mix of what she wants or what she fears than what she actually sees. Her psychic abilities are actually better with strangers than with the people she loves. I've heard that's not un-common.

"What I'm seeing," Jan continues whether I like it or not, "is this woman being in a blind rage toward you. I see her doing everything in her power to hurt you, includ-ing coming after your girls." Jan's voice cracks. "This woman is bad news. Whatever you do, don't you let her touch you."

Okay, I'm not smiling anymore. Lady Dragon's never been in a ritual for me, including my Initiation and previous Elevation to Second Degree. But she insists on being in the ritual in the Elevation for all Third Degrees and part of that ritual means that she will lay hands on my shoulders and pass to me the power that was passed on to her as it was passed on from her High Priestess as it was passed on by her High Priestess as it was passed on by her High Priest as it was passed on by his High Priest as it was passed on by Gerald Gardner. All the members of that lineage were distinguished and well-known in the community.

In the Elevation ritual, from what I had heard of the part that isn't oathbound—or must not be if Donna and the Elders thought it was okay to tell me—Lady Dragon and at least some of the Elders will all lay their hands on me and pass power on to me, and when I walk out of that ritual, I will be so pumped with energy that my aura will glow for the next month or more, and I'll feel like I can do anything and everything. I'll feel like there's no stopping me, and according to Donna, that's going to be great for dealing with Quent and starting my life over.

"Lauren, this woman has a lot of issues, a lot of bad issues, negative things. You don't need her energy. You don't need her touching you. Whatever you do, do *not* let her touch you. Not only that, but you're going to have to shield. She is psychic and a lot of people around her will be psychic, and you'll have to shield to make sure they don't see this dilemma you're in. If they do, then they're going to move in and try to manipulate you so it won't be a matter of free choice. She'll work magick to make sure you stay with her. Do you understand?"

"I understand, Jan. I know, but it's going to be all right. If I'm supposed to be there, I'll be there."

"So I can't talk you out of it?"

"No, Jan."

She sighs again, heavier this time than before. "Okay, well, I love you. You be careful, okay?"

"Okay, love you, too."

I put my phone away and when I look up again I see a pair of crows circling the clinic next door. *One crow, sorrow. Two crows, mirth.* Then my gaze drops to a convertible skidding into the parking lot. Dr. Matthews.

I check my watch. It's 8:20 a.m. His office opens at 8 a.m. He's late for work.

He barely pulls the key out of the ignition before his door's open and he's bounding out. He pauses at the employee entrance and looks up at the sky, smiling, sunshine on his face.

I glimpse a vision of him on the water, sun on his face, but it vanishes as quickly as I see it. The vision startles me, but in it, he's happy even though he's all alone.

Another crow calls and circles overhead. *Three crows, a wedding.* A second later, the fourth crow appears and joins the circle. *Four crows. Birth.*

The crows are so often around him. Why?

Then another crow and another. At least a dozen crows in the sky above the clinic as Dr. Matthews disappears into the clinic. Then another dozen. They circle and land. Some on the rooftop, some in the trees, one on the handrail outside the employee entrance.

"It's going to be okay," I tell myself. The Goddess has sent me a sign. All those crows. It's going to be okay. Regardless of what happens today, I'm going to be protected.

My plane lands at Dulles airport outside Washington a few minutes after midnight. I've already missed the Thursday night opening ritual at the Grand Coven meeting at a State Park several hours away, but from my window in the sky, I've looked down at the white, fluffy swirls of Tropical Storm Bonnie. I looked into its eye as the plane waited until the storm passed, then we flew over the storm, and now we've landed ahead of it. Although Bonnie came through my own backyard, it's ironically expected to follow me all the way to Maryland to stall out there and dump rain for days, possibly threatening the weekend rituals.

Bone-weary, I step into the receiving area. I have only one small suitcase, my carry-on, so I don't need to go to the luggage counter.

A strawberry blonde in a sea of empty chairs glances up from an Anne Rice novel. Her eyes light up and she jumps up, waving her arms. "Raven! Rav— Lauren! Over here!"

We embrace and I think that I could fall asleep right here and now. I am so tired. But I have much to talk to Donna about. The one thing I can't talk to her about yet is my decision about staying with Dragon Hart Grand Coven or leaving it. I can't talk to her about it because I still don't know.

"You're walking better," Donna notices, taking my suitcase from me and wheeling it behind her. A former ballerina, she's several years younger than me, a little on the anorexic side, and bounces along beside me as I walk somewhat more cautiously through the terminal. "Did you see the doctor?" she asks.

"Yes, two days ago, but he didn't do anything for me."

I feel myself blush and don't tell her that I entertained a brief sexual fantasy about him last night before reminding myself that he's married and ten years my junior. I haven't had fantasies of any other man in years, so I was surprised that thoughts of him popped into my head in a moment of lustful loneliness, particularly from a chance meeting with him several years ago in the pasta aisle at the grocery story when he'd been hiding his biceps and chest under a close-fitting red, cable-knit sweater. It wasn't even a recent image of him. Gods, I don't want to be one of those insane women who has fantasies about her physician, even though his style is so low-key that I don't think of him as some kind of power figure to yearn for or some life-wielding savior.

"He hasn't done anything for the condition," I correct myself. "Not yet, anyway. I've postponed my physical therapy until the end of the month when I can take some time off from work."

"So he gave you medicine or—?"

"No, nothing. We agreed to take a more homeopathic approach. He offered me anti-inflammatories, but I said no. I'd rather not take any medicines if I can help it."

"But you are walking better. I mean a little slow," she teases, "but nothing like I had imagined."

I laugh. "Well, this is nothing like it was. I don't know what happened, but almost overnight my knees have gotten better. I was afraid they'd keep me from making this trip."

"No, Lauren. You're meant to be here."

We find her orange SUV and she helps me inside. My knees still make a funny grinding noise as I sit down, but it doesn't seem to hurt right now. I note the tents in plastic storage boxes she has in the back of her vehicle.

"Have you heard from Lady Dragon? Is she upset that I'm not there yet?"

Donna shrugs and says nothing else until we're out on the highway. "I haven't heard a word. Technically you don't have to be there until your Elevation ritual starts. I had told her, as well as the other Elders, that you were having trouble leaving Florida because of the storms. All Dragon would say at the time was that if you're meant to be at the Grand Coven gathering, you will be."

I'm not sure how to answer that. I've heard the same sentiment before, but usually in regard to someone who was supposed to be part of an open ritual and, at the last minute, sprained their ankle and had to sit it out. Lady Dragon had remarked then that sometimes Spirit knows best and that that person obviously, for whatever reason, was not meant to participate in that ritual. Though I do agree with that philosophy, there's something about the way Donna stated Lady Dragon's comment that doesn't sit well in the pit of my stomach.

"Donna, does Lady Dragon know what my Third Degree challenge is? Did you tell her?"

"Er, no. No, and you're not to say a word, either. I'll tell her when the time is right. Well, I mean I'll tell her what the challenge is. You'll tell her whether you're staying or not. I can't do that for you. Only you can."

"Donna?" I turn halfway in my seat to look at the road sign we just passed. "I thought we were going to the coven gathering tonight. That sign back there said—"

"No, not tonight. We'll go in the morning." Then she narrows her eyes at me. "There is no way in hell that I'm going to drive several hours and then spend another hour setting up a tent. No, we're going to Barbara's house in Brunswick instead. She lives only an hour or so from here, and Deedee and Mariah are with her tonight, waiting for us. Sarah, Beverly, and the others are at the State Park already."

"Three of them are at Barbara's instead of at the Grand Coven meeting?" I don't understand. "How did they get out of that? I thought it was mandatory for all Elders."

"All current Elders." Donna kicks at the accelerator. We're doing 85 m.p.h. on the open highway, and I'm feeling really glad I'm protected by the Goddess right now.

"Of all the Elders," Donna continues, "half of them have already quit or been kicked out. When Barbara and DeeDee were told that their Eldership was being taken away, they quit on the spot. They reminded Dragon of what she said about how you get your Elevations from Spirit and not from man. Spirit gives and only Spirit can take it away. Barbara and DeeDee told Dragon she couldn't take it away, to which our esteemed leader answered maybe she couldn't take it away from them altogether, but she could take it away under the auspices of the Dragon Hart Grand Coven. So they could still be Elders, just Elders somewhere else."

"And Mariah?"

"Mariah was kicked out three weeks ago for not showing Dragon the proper respect."

I grinned. "Used the F-word to her face, huh?"

"You got it."

"So why are the three of them together tonight waiting for us?"

"Not for us. For *you*."

Three Elders are waiting for me. I shake my head. I've seen these women in ritual. I know the kind of power that reverberates off them. All three women individually amaze me. Together, they mortify me.

"I've told them about your challenge. And that it's your choice and that you'll make up your mind over this weekend. I also told them what you said about deciding you didn't want Dragon to touch you."

I'd relayed the message to Donna while I'd waited for my second flight in Atlanta.

"What did they say?" They probably thought I was crazy. Everyone who is a Third Degree in Dragon Hart has had the power passed on to them directly from Lady Dragon herself.

"There is an option," Donna says, her voice low even though it's only the two of us in the SUV. It's almost as if she's afraid Lady Dragon will hear. "You're not going to like it, but it is an option."

"I'm open."

She glances at me and smiles. "Yeah, you are, aren't you! In the three years I've known you, I've never seen you this open." She laughs. "Okay, well, here's the option. There is no way you're going to get through an Elevation of this level without Dragon touching you. However, Mariah has a copy of the Third Degree ritual. All you need is three Elders to perform it. And tonight, we've got four who are willing."

We sit in silence while I think about it. If they conduct my ritual at Barbara's, then there are certain members of the Grand Coven who won't be able to attend, like Leo for example. Still, after what I've learned about Lady Dragon and what Jan told me this morning, I can't fathom allowing that woman to touch me or pass any of her tainted energy to me.

"Okay, so what happens if we do it tonight instead of tomorrow? Do we get to the Grand Coven meeting and announce that 'Hey, here's Lady RavenHart, a new Third Degree, and you didn't have anything to say about it'?"

"She's already given approval. She gave approval of you as a Third Degree candidate when she signed off on your exam. Worst case is, you go through the Elevation twice. Except this time, you'll have the protection of the Third Degree around you."

"And she won't know that? I mean will she be able to tell it in my aura?"

Donna swallows hard. "There was a time when she could have. She used to have that gift, but not anymore. At least, not in a long, long time."

Lady Dragon lost one of her gifts? No one has ever really talked to me before about Third Degrees and Elders losing their gifts, just *getting* their gifts. It is said that no one but Spirit can give these talents to them, whether it is for healing or knowing or whatever it might be. The flip side, I thought, is only Spirit can take them away.

"So she won't try to take away my Third Degree if I decide to leave?"

"She can't take your Third Degree. Only Spirit gives the Third Degree and only Spirit can take it away and, as Dragon is fond of saying, no one has any right to say whether you've earned your Elevation or not because they haven't walked in your shoes—and that includes Dragon. What you've got to decide is whether you want to be 'Thirded' at a Grand Coven meeting or do you want to be 'Thirded' by a small group of Elders?"

"It's the same ritual, right?"

"Yes."

"And the same results, right?"

"Yes."

"Except that if I get my Third at the Grand Coven meeting where Lady Dragon will be, then Lady Dragon will infuse me with her energy. Am I right?"

"You're right."

I take a deep breath and start to speak. I can't. I take another deep breath. "Then let's do it tonight."

That was easy, easier than I expected. It just feels *right*. I would never have accepted this three years ago and always looked forward to having Lady Dragon in the circle with me at my Third. And now, it is so easy to say no. For the first time in my life, it is becoming easy to say no. The Third Degree transformation is beginning already.

"Okay, then. Tonight it is. And in the morning, we'll go over to the Grand Coven meeting and you can decide if you want to go through the ritual again, and you can answer the challenge if you're ready. You won't really feel the effects of the Third until your challenge has been answered. But whatever you do, under whatever circumstances, do not mention the mission to Dragon."

Did she mean the Center of Light? "Her mission or mine?"

"Same thing." Donna reaches for the radio, and I know she'll say nothing more.

Having met Barbara twice before, I'd always pictured her house as being a tiny white cottage. Instead it is a rambling farm house on the outskirts of Frederick, Maryland, with a strong hint of Amish. I can't see much of the house except the lights—one in every first and second story window. Barbara is having company tonight, obviously. On this moonless night, I can see the outline of the barn against the utility light in the backyard. And I hear horses whinnying restlessly as I step out of the orange SUV.

Three Elders are waiting on the front porch. Candles, burned down to various stages, are scattered around the porch with a couple of decks of Tarot cards and a handful of rune stones in their midst.

Barbara and DeeDee are both my age, maybe a few years older. The lines are beginning to show in their faces, and conservative hair styles and eyeglasses that make them look more like stereotypical librarians than stereotypical witches.

Mariah is younger, in her thirties with blue hair and a nose ring, probably the youngest of the Elders and the most recent, but she's been a member of the Grand Coven since she was a teenager. She Initiated young. Probably about the time she was Rhiannon's age. During her college years alone, she brought at least five new covens into the Grand Coven. All of them have been thriving, and one is still vibrant on the college campus she left years ago. Of the covens she spawned, they've bred many more within the Dragon Hart Grand Coven. Fully a third of the Grand Coven's members are her legacies.

Her current boyfriend, a twenty-something with hair dyed black and hanging in his eyes, sits on the porch swing and rocks back and forth. He is a Third Degree of the Dragon Hart as well, though I suspect he won't be much longer, not if Mariah's been kicked out.

"They see your shininess and they don't want to leave you," Mariah had told me once. She'd shrugged. "It's the bane of all High Priestesses. They can see the Goddess coming through you, and they want a part of it."

After an uneasy exchange of hugs, the six of us settle down on the floor of the porch.

"I've decided what I'm going to do," I announce rather loudly.

Barbara holds up a hand, then walks out into the yard. She stands silently, facing North.

"Oooh, pretty," I hear Payne, Mariah's boyfriend, say behind me.

I know then what Barbara's done. She's cast a circle, one of protection, around us. Payne's visual. He has that gift; I don't. I can feel the circle around us, like the wings of a crow around me. But I can't see it.

Barbara comes back and sits on the top step and looks up at me. "What, sweetheart? What have you decided?"

"I want to go ahead to do the ritual tonight." I glance from Elder to Elder and then to Payne. "I don't want to wait, and I don't want Lady Dragon to touch me tomorrow."

Donna nods. "The power was passed down to all of us, not just from Dragon, but we all also had her High Priestess in our Third Degrees Elevations and in our Elderings. So the power was passed on directly from her High Priestess as well." Donna laughs, but it comes out a little hollow, a little worried. "Raven would still get the full dose."

"No," Barbara says. Donna and I look at each other, then back at Barbara. Grimness shrouds her face. "We can't do it tonight."

"Tomorrow morning?" I ask hopefully.

Barbara shakes her head. "I mean, we can't do it. It's going to have to be tomorrow, at the Grand Coven meeting, and unfortunately Dragon's going to have to be part of it. But don't worry, we'll think of something."

"But it's okay with me to do it tonight."

"No, it has to be tomorrow." Barbara gestures at a Celtic cross spread of Tarot cards on the floor. The only one I can make out in the dimness is the Queen of Swords.

There's a heaviness in her voice when she speaks again. "You have to do it tomorrow. There's something you're going to get out of doing it there that you won't get out of doing it here. I don't know what it is, but it has to be there."

Donna sits back against one of the pillars on the porch and leans her head against its white plaster. "How are we ever going to keep Dragon from touching her? Barb, what are we going to do?"

"We? I'm not even going to be there. Those who are not active members of Dragon Hart are not allowed to be present at any of this weekend's activities, remember? In fact, you might want to get a hotel for tomorrow night because, Donna, as soon as you tell her you're leaving and the other Elders are leaving, you'll have to go. And if our Raven chooses to stay, she'll have to have a taxi come pick her up to take her to the airport, because you won't be allowed back."

"That's ridiculous," I sputter.

DeeDee grins back at me. "That's our Dragon."

"Look, she's not going to make a big deal out of this, is she? I mean, if she can get rid of all the Elders and leave it up to you and tell you that it's your choice whether to stay or go, then why is she going to be upset about me leaving?"

They exchange silent looks and chuckle, but say nothing more.

"Tell them about the mission," Donna says.

Everyone is silent, their eyes on me. I've never heard such a hush.

"Um, okay. I have this feeling that the Goddess wants me to put together this certain project. It's a big project. Um, there are these Centers of Light. They're like healing centers or learning centers and—"

Already Barbara, Mariah, and DeeDee exchange glances. Payne sits up straight.

"—And they're all under this big pagan umbrella, though it's not necessarily pagan. It's spiritual, but it's definitely not Judaeo-Christian. But we're all under this one big umbrella, all these different covens and churches and groups and every pagan and New Age spiritual-type person who wants to be under it can, and they can get group medical insurance under this organization or they can get access to lessons, uh…mentorship, exchanging workshops, scholarships, uh…just all these resources and—" I stop. "What's wrong?"

Barbara wrings her hands. "Oh, shit. Shit, shit, shit." She looks up, then reaches over and touches me on the knee. "Honey, even if you wanted to, Dragon's never going to let you leave."

7

It's over. I'm a Third Degree now.

And I am so utterly disappointed.

Donna says I'm free to tell what happened if I want. The others have been told it's all oathbound. I don't understand what's different about me and I don't plan to say anything anyway. Though I wish I could tell Jan that yes, there was a group in black robes chanting around me but it wasn't what she'd thought. Nor was the worry that I was bleeding.

The energy around me feels fried, chaotic. Lady Dragon and a select group of Third Degrees—most of them police detectives and Marines—have erected a sphere of energy around the camp site to keep out trouble and to hold energy inside. I'm told that I'll feel content as long as I'm in the sphere but may be a little antsy once I leave it and the "group mind." For now, the most obvious effect of the energy amplification is that at least half of the women have unexpectedly ended their menstrual cycles and the others swear they're ovulating. Not that it matters, but I'm in the first group. So Jan was right that I was bleeding.

Famished, I stand in the food tent. Other new Third Degrees wander in and out. All of us have the munchies now. I sit by myself in one corner and stare out into the dark woods where the blackness is broken occasionally by the flash of a firefly. A symphony of locusts, crickets, and frogs resounds through the night as I sip an ice-cold can of Pepsi and crunch Nacho Cheese Doritos in rhythm with the frogs. It'll be daylight soon.

"Darling, congratulations."

Tyler appears out of nowhere and hugs me from behind. He smells of dragon's blood incense, just like that package containing the dirt on Lady Dragon. I relax into Tyler's arms and let him hug me. I like openly gay men, their sense of style, their sense of humor, their sense of artistry. I like everything about openly gay men, except for their sexual preference. Otherwise, I've met a few that I would consider damned near perfect.

Tyler's much shorter than his partner, Leo, and his long hair is as blond as Leo's is black. And Leo always smells of patchouli. They live in the fashionable side of New York City and though they're not exactly wealthy, they never miss a Broadway show.

He gives me a kiss on the cheek and then on the back of my neck. "I'm so proud of you, darling. You did so well."

"Thanks, Tyler, and thanks for everything you did for me tonight." I don't say what, not out loud, but he knows what I mean. He just smiles and winks at me, and I'm grateful the exception was made to allow him back into the circle, even if it was only because of Leo's pleading with Lady Dragon. Tyler's not so much a part of the group anymore but he's been allowed to come and go. That's an exception to the rule. Perhaps because of the issue with his artwork being confiscated.

Tonight's Elevation ritual was different, from what I've been told. Each Elevation ritual takes anywhere between one to two hours, depending on the candidate and how they answer the questions posed to them. This year, since we had twenty-one Second Degrees Elevating to Third, Lady Dragon had made a decision for everyone to do the ritual at the exact same time. We would all be ritual-mates and all bonded together for the rest of our lives, having gone through the same ceremony and made the same pledges to the same Gods to continue the tradition of Dragon Hart.

And although I'd been right there in the middle of all those candidates, what Lady Dragon did not see was that I had not taken the same pledges. Thanks to Donna, Leo, Tyler, Payne, and two other Elders who had cast a circle over me within the larger circle to protect me from the influences around me. Instead, I took my vows to teach others about The Morrigan and Herne, rather than bringing new members into Dragon Hart as though it were a spiritual pyramid scheme.

This year, unlike other years, Lady Dragon did not lay her hands on each candidate and pass power individually to each candidate, only to a few and to her own children—the twin boys who were going off to college and, she thought, needed a little extra power boost. Their presence at the ritual had surprised me. That two boys that young could be so ready, shortly after their eighteenth birthdays? That they could be so ready to take on the responsibility of pagan clergy troubled and surprised me. Neither was the model of maturity, even for a pair of skateboarding teens.

"Where's Leo?" I ask, suddenly aware that Tyler is alone in the food tent with me. I turn to face Tyler. "Is Leo all right? He seemed happy during the ritual, but before and right after…."

"He's sad, darling. If you must know, he's on the verge of falling apart."

"Why?"

I adore Leo. He is always so happy, so calm, so relaxed. He has a way of going to this happy place in his head when he meditates, a way of communing with the Ether with such delight that most people, just looking at him, would think he's high. And in a way, he usually is.

Not since I saw him today when I first arrived at the campground, though. He seemed to get a little bit of that ethereal glow back during the ritual. Actually he seemed to be himself during the whole ritual. Afterward, the glow turned to sadness again.

All he would say was, "Sometimes, sweetness, it's a real pain in the ass to be clairvoyant." Then he'd added, "I prefer not to know everything that's going to happen this weekend, so instead, I'm just not going to think about it. Not yet, anyway. There'll be time enough later."

"And where's the illustrious Lady Lynx?" Tyler asks, meaning Donna. I don't often hear her magickal name.

Tyler's voice hints at a lilt as if he realizes I'm disturbed and he's trying to cheer me up. I glance at my watch—it's almost five in the morning. Sunrise will be coming soon. I haven't slept all night. We haven't even pitched a tent. I'm drained from the Elevation ceremony and yet I'm so pumped with energy I'll probably be able to go the next three days without sleeping. Everyone's like that, except for the new Dedicants…and the First Degrees and Second Degrees. Hmmm. In other words, only the ones who attended the Third Degree Elevation are feeling this particular stimulant.

"Donna went to find Lady Dragon."

"Oh." Tyler bites at his lip. "Is everything okay?"

I shrug. "I'm not sure. Donna needed to talk to her when we arrived. Lady Dragon hasn't had five minutes to spare for her yet today, so she had to wait until after the ritual tonight."

The fact is, Lady Dragon has put Donna off three times already since we arrived at the campground. Donna asked to speak privately to Lady Dragon. Each time, Lady Dragon had two to three Third Degrees hovering around her. Almost like bodyguards.

Donna finally said, "Look, I need to speak to you in private. You know what it's about, I know what it's about, and they don't need to know."

At that, Lady Dragon had agreed but told Donna she would have to wait until after the ritual tonight. After the ritual, Lady Dragon had put her off yet again. She needed to do something else first and she would summon Donna when she was ready to talk to her. I've seen Donna get perturbed and impatient with other people, and I can tell it's there just under the surface with Lady Dragon, but Donna doesn't mention it.

I don't understand why Lady Dragon kept postponing her conversation with Donna. She knows that Donna is going to tell her she's leaving. I'm sure of that. It's also clear that she welcomes Donna's leaving, that she doesn't want Donna to be part of the group anymore. She doesn't want her to be an Elder, and she really doesn't want her to be around at all. She wants new followers, fresh followers. Ones who aren't used up.

So why make Donna wait? It is almost like it's some kind of game, or…or manipulation.

I've already decided after reading several articles on "how to tell if your coven was really a cult," that while Dragon Hart does have some disturbing new developments in the past two years, it isn't a cult after all. Not yet, anyway. Not as long as it has a check and balance of Elders. Not as long as it doesn't force people to stay. Not as long as it allows for a free flow of communication with families and with people who don't necessarily agree with Dragon Hart. In spite of its leader, the group itself is a good one and the training has been excellent.

Will I leave or stay? I still don't know. I'm still waiting for Spirit to come whisper in my ear, *Stay* or *Go.*

Or even *Stay if you will, go if you must.* But something, some kind of sign. A vision, some kind of anything to help me make the right decision.

I've faced this before, back with Belinda when she left. She never could tell me exactly why, but she's not the kind of person to do things lightly, especially as much as she loved Dragon Hart. I'd taken a few days to give Belinda my answer of whether I would stay with Dragon Hart or go with her to start a new group, one where I would have been Elevated much faster. I hadn't needed several days to make up my mind. I'd known almost from the moment she told me that she was leaving and that I had a choice of coming with her, that I would not go. That Dragon Hart was where I was supposed to be.

I didn't know why then. I do know why now. It's because of the training and, too, because of some of the people I've met. Donna for one, Leo with tales of The Treat for another. Leo helped me so much in getting through my divorce, plus giving me hope for new things to come into my life. I never would have had that if I had left with Belinda.

This time is different. This time I don't hear Spirit sitting on my shoulder saying, *Stay.* I don't hear Spirit saying, *Go*, either. I want a sign, need a sign. I'm like that. I like signs. I like big honking billboards that tell me exactly what to do and clearly enough that even I, an idiot, can understand. And such have been the words of my prayers many a time: "Give me a sign. One that even I can recognize."

It's my Third Degree challenge, and I have to make up my mind at some point. Maybe I'm supposed to decide without the help of Spirit. It seems kind of silly to me because I want the help of Spirit with everything in my life. Why would I deny it with such a major decision?

"Hmm." Tyler gives a little grunt of appreciation as Chevron, another new Third Degree, wonders through the food tent. Tyler notes his momentary lapse and catches himself. "Sorry, darling. I can still look, can't I? Not that I'd ever dream of straying from Leo, but I can appreciate the sight of something exquisite. Besides, I really think Chev is more to your type than mine."

I don't disagree, but I'm not so sure of that either. Yes, Chevron is most definitely straight. He's also single, a widower from what Donna has said. But I don't think he's The Treat. He looks, however, exactly as Jan has described as my ideal man.

"I think you're going to meet someone on this trip," she told me just a few days ago. "I think you're going to meet The Treat while you're at your Grand Coven thingie."

She went on to describe the man she saw as my perfect match. And the man in front of me, chowing down on pretzels and soda while he gazes out into the dark woods, is a physical embodiment of what she's foreseen. A big guy, not fat, but a teddy bear sort of physique. Short dark hair with a touch of gray at the temples. A few years older than I am. He walks with a ceremonial staff, one he used in ritual tonight to cast his circle. He is handsome, interesting to talk to for the few minutes I've been in his presence, and exudes a warm energy. But there isn't anything particularly enchanting about him. In some ways, he reminds me of a younger version of Jan's husband. And perhaps, just perhaps, the man she envisions for me is really the one she envisions for herself as perfect. Jan's like that when it comes to my romantic life and prophecies. She wants for me what she wants for herself, what she believes she already has in creating her own happy world.

Chevron downs the rest of his soda, throws away his pretzel bag, and then upon hearing distant strains of "We All Come from the Goddess," breaks out into song himself and wonders off to join the other revelers.

Tyler describes the present he can't wait to give me, the one he's left back at his and Leo's tent. It's a Third Degree basket, as he calls it, a portable ritual kit with candles for fire, incense for air, quartz crystals for earth, and some seashells for water. There's a bottle of dragon's blood oil as well and a small altar cloth of purple with a pentagram in the center of it. He made the basket himself out of grape vines he grew on his mother's farm in upstate New York. It's a gift of love, all for my Third Degree.

Leo, on the other hand, doesn't make things. He's not gifted at that, he says. His gift to me will be another reading. A reading that I'm hoping to receive tonight, except that I don't know where Leo is. Since the ritual ended, he's been gone on an uncharacteristic walk into the woods and down to the lake. Even more uncharacteristic, he insisted that his lover stay behind because Leo needed time alone. Considering the accuracy of his clairvoyance, that doesn't seem to be a good thing.

Tyler gives me another hug, plucks a single Cheeto from an open bag on the table, and follows Chevron into the night, singing softly something that sounds like the Pretenders' "Hymn to Her."

I'm alone in the food tent now, still wearing my ritual robe and a thick sheen of perspiration from all the energy I've expended through the night. I was told exactly how I would feel when this Elevation was done, like I could walk on water, like I couldn't stop laughing, like I could do anything. And yet, it isn't there. It just isn't there.

What's wrong? Did the ritual not "take"? I'm still energized, yes, but it isn't the way it's been described to me. It's like… it's like something's missing. Is this all there is?

"Raven!" shrills Butterfly Moonbeam behind me. "Butterfuck" as Donna always calls her. "Wasn't that just the best?" She walks in front of me and twirls, arms to the sky. She accidentally topples a battery-powered lantern.

"Isn't it wonderful? Oh, that was so amazing! Have you ever felt this way before?"

Her eyes gleam. She twirls again. Her ritual gown is one that was designed and made especially for her and probably cost several hundred dollars. It's black, as required by our tradition, but in a pretty burned-out velvet mixed with satin and silk. It's a frilly concoction of goth corset and medieval bell sleeves with a fairy skirt. She wears spike heels with it, the kind that make my knees ache just to look at them. I'm still not sure how she managed to stand up straight and cast her circle tonight.

She's my age with two daughters the same ages as mine. Sonnet and her younger daughter have the same birthday and they sometimes email each other, though they've never met. We've talked often over the years, mainly by email. I met her daughters once, first year I was with Dragon Hart, and they were adorable. Polite, well-behaved, loving, as bubbly as Butterfly herself. Though she lived in California at the time, she and her daughters had traveled to a Renaissance faire near Baltimore while attending Grand Coven events and had met a ceremonial magician from Washington, D.C. Three months later, she declared him to be the love of her life, gave up custody of her daughters to an abusive ex in Redondo Beach, and moved to Frederick, Maryland to be with her new love and take care of his four motherless daughters.

I didn't understand that. I could never give up my children and I would never leave them behind. But as she announced earlier today, she's happy with her new family and she got through her Second Degree just fine and here she is now, dancing and singing in front of me, a new Third Degree. It's not my place to judge what she's been through, but I just can't understand it.

Still, it's much better tonight listening to her chatter on and on about the ritual and how it affected her versus what her lover did last week and what her lover's going to do next week and what he thinks about all these different things as if she didn't have a thought in her own head as to what she might think about anything. There's evidence, too, of a crack in their foundation. He's become slightly less enamored of her, now that his kids are a few years older and aren't quite so needy of a wet-nurse figure. Truthfully, I'm surprised their relationship has lasted through her Second Degree. I've been told often that anything new that comes into your life during your Second, you shouldn't try to hang onto because it won't last. It's all part of the transition process.

"Jonny! Jonny, over here," Butterfly squeals and waves at a new Third Degree whom I don't know. I've never seen him before the ritual tonight, so if he was at previous Grand Coven meetings, I never noticed him. He's from somewhere in Montana. Jonny is a large man, well over six feet tall, and built like a mountain.

They chat for awhile, forgetting that I'm there, while Jonny makes a ham and cheese sandwich and fetches a fresh bottle of water from the cooler. He's eating healthier than the rest of us. Feeling slightly disconnected, I listen to their banter, their self-congratulations as well as their congratulations to each other.

"Oh, Jonny, could you just believe it when Lady Dragon asked us to call the Quarters in unison?"

I smile to myself. I know what she's talking about. We'd been a hodge-podge of energy with around twenty Third Degree candidates in the midst of the circle, casting our own circles and calling the Quarters, all at the same time, just to save time and be efficient. I hadn't been so nervous as I'd expected. Suddenly, everything had just felt right. And as everyone else tried to remember the Quarter calls and the Official Circle Casting and say them all in unison, in what turned out to be a cacophony of sound and energy, I had held my circle steady. I had closed my eyes and stopped talking, no longer even moving my lips to speak the casting or the calls, but rather intoning them in my head, visualizing, feeling. And knowing that it was done.

"I know," Jonny says. "Wasn't that amazing? I've never heard anything like that."

Butterfly nods. "Disgusting, wasn't it? I mean these people are supposed to be Third Degree candidates and they can't even deliver the correct circle casting or Quarter calls."

Jonny drinks from his water bottle and then nods. "Obviously there is some flaw in the uniformity of the teachings of this organization."

I blink at him. Did I hear right? It was all about using the correct words? And saying them with the correct phrasing and pronunciation? No, I didn't remember that being part of the laws of magick or universal laws or any other laws. One thing I have discovered for myself in my training is that getting the exact word and the exact phrase and the exact pronunciation, the exact pause for dramatic breath before performance—which is what some people tried to make it, a *performance*—doesn't really matter. What matters is intent. And energy. When I work my magick, I work it not to *perform* for other people, but for the Gods and for myself and, with permission, for others. It isn't about the performance. It is about the connection with Deity.

"I'm just thankful that I had such a wonderful teacher," Butterfly continues. "I would have been so embarrassed if I had done what others did tonight, you know, delivering the wrong Quarter call. You know that Quarter call tonight? Half the people were saying one that was on page five of the very first lesson and that's not the one we're supposed to give. After we become a Second Degree, we're supposed to use the Official Quarter Call and Official Circle Casting that's on the tenth page of Lesson Number Seven."

I smile to myself. Ah, yes, that's why Butterfly earned the highest score this year on the test. She knows exactly where to find the right words, but does she have the energy? I'm seeing a side to her I've never seen before. She's always been a bit giddy, flighty, fluff-bunny, but tonight, as of the ritual, there is a harshness in her voice. It's sometimes said that Third Degrees can be really full of themselves for the first thirty days because they feel the power that's been passed to them. They feel the rawness of it, and it brings out things that were only barely there before.

I don't like this side of Butterfly. I don't like what I'm seeing now. She's so caught up in the performance that I can't even sense her spirituality right now.

But Jonny agrees with her and even expresses his concern over the future of the organization, especially if our High Priests and High Priestesses can't remember the correct Quarter calls to give and how to say them with a loud, clear voice that can be heard above all the others.

I wonder if their snarkiness has anything to do with the fact that Lady Dragon did actually touch them both in the passing of power. Most people, she hadn't. I had been one of the fortunate ones, fortunate because she had missed me in the crowd. She'd been too attuned to her own children. I'd commented to Jenna, one of the Elders, on how amazed I was that two boys just graduating from high school could already be getting their Third Degrees. That meant that they had probably started when they were younger than Rhiannon. It shocked me that two eighteen-year-olds would be that mature, particularly those two boys.

Jenna had laughed. "They didn't go through a degree program like you, Raven. Where did you get that idea?"

"Well, because they were being Elevated tonight."

"No, sweetheart. Don't you think for one minute that they went through what you've gone through in the past how many years? Five?"

"Three," I corrected.

"Oh, okay, three years. That's quick. Sheesh, that's more like getting hit with the Tower Card than the Death Card. Three years, well, that's sudden, abrupt change, not just an old way of life dying and new beginnings. Pretty rough, wasn't it?"

I nodded.

"No, sweetheart. Those boys of Dragon's? They didn't go through the program you did. Their mama just decided that she wanted to make sure that they were going off to college empowered and with a string on them so she could pull them back, if necessary."

Hoots and hollers break out again on the other side of the campground. Butterfly and Jonny look up from their conversation, grin, shrug, and return to what they were saying.

Then Butterfly cocks her head. "I don't see the moon out anywhere."

"Because it's a dark moon night," I murmur.

"Dark moon," Jonny informs her without hearing me. "Plus Mercury is in retrograde."

And two hurricanes passing over Florida and headed this way.

It's said that Lady Dragon has a way of manifesting things. She simply puts out the word to the Universe to keep away anyone who would cause her consternation. And that it's been known before that certain storms and catastrophes and personal disasters have kept people away. At least that's the word she's put out.

Earlier today, when she saw me and told me she was looking forward to my Third Degree Elevation to-night, she said not to bring those hurricanes with me. She said it in a harsh tone that had surprised me and yet was still joking. But there was an undertone that maybe she wasn't joking. Yes, the hurricanes had followed me there, but I had a feeling it was more like a boomerang effect, especially after things the Elders had told me last night.

"What's that mean?" Butterfly asks. She'd always had a look of confusion on her face, but this one is a little bit more pronounced.

"Mercury in retrograde and a dark moon—not the most auspicious time to get your Third Degree," I murmur again under my breath, quoting something Mariah said.

Jonny stops smiling and lowers his head, bending in to her. I can barely hear him. "What do you mean, 'what does that mean?'"

"I mean, what does it mean?"

Jonny looks uncomfortable. "You know, like in the Astrology Lesson, Lesson Number Eighteen."

Butterfly gives her usual little titter of a laugh, like she is perpetually nervous. Maybe she is. "I didn't take the Astrology Lesson. Lady Dragon told me I didn't have to."

"What?" I can't help it. The word just comes crashing out of me. "What do you mean you didn't take the lesson?"

The Astrology Lesson is well-known among all Dragon Hart Third Degrees to be the absolute roughest of the bunch. Because of a bookkeeping glitch, I'd received my lesson only three days before I took my final exam, and I damned near killed myself cramming for it. Just about every question I had missed on the exam came from the astrology section, which comprised at least a third of the entire exam, largely because Lady Dragon is an astrologer of some repute and has an internationally known website that sells computer-generated reports cheaply to generate leads for very expensive personal consultations.

And Butterfly had gotten out of taking the worst of the exam? She'd been exempt? Favorites had been played?

"Why?" I don't know whether to ask how or why or what. I just can't believe it. The Astrology Lesson was so hard and the material was so difficult to understand—to a degree of being a professional astrologer, which is what you were expected to be once you finished the exam. Various covens within Dragon Hart occasionally take up collections and have Lady Dragon flown to a coven meeting so that they can learn personally from her everything they need to know to pass the exam.

And yet Butterfly had gotten out of the exam!

She looks a little flustered, then says, "I.... Don't... don't say anything, okay? I'm not supposed to tell anybody. Nobody's supposed to know that."

Yeah, right. Like Butterfly can keep a secret?

Jonny crosses his arms. "I overheard Chevron say that he'd heard Merewynn and Bonita talking about somebody rumored to have gotten out of parts of the exam. But they didn't think it was so."

Butterfly puts her fingers to her lips. "Oops. Yeah, I did say something in front of Bonita's sister."

My throat tightens. I can't help but think of three sleepless nights I spent cramming material, not understanding any of it well enough to hold onto it enough after the exam. And of the three nights that I hadn't had time to spend with my kids because I'd been working on that and Quent had been in one of his yelling frenzies.

"How...why did you get exempt and others didn't?" I ask.

"I-I just seemed to have a mental block to it, you know? Astrology's just not my thing."

"Yeah, it wasn't mine, either, but I didn't know I had a choice." Lady Dragon seriously fancies herself as a professional astrologer and she's always been picky about insisting that everyone in her group have the same abilities or have the same gift or a similar talent to hers regardless of whether that student has an aptitude for that particular form of divination. Except that, according to the emails in the package that smelled like dragon's blood, she always has to be better at the gifts than anyone else.

Jonny shrugs. "Well, to be honest with you, I have heard of other people getting out of certain lessons so that they could get their Third Degree Elevation within the allotted seven years' time to do it."

He may have heard it, but I hadn't. It makes me wonder, though, about the criteria for a cult. I'd already decided even before talking to the Elders last night that Dragon Hart probably did not qualify as a cult though I thought it did have some potential danger areas. Until now, I hadn't known of Lady Dragon granting any special favors, but apparently favors were there for the granting for certain people.

Donna had specifically asked for my Astrology Lesson to be waived, given that I don't have any need of it and don't show any particular aptitude for it and didn't get the lesson in time to study properly before my final exam. According to Donna, I was given a resounding *No!* And yet Butterfly, asking for the same thing, had been granted leniency.

Something about this jangles at my fairness meter.

Donna appears at my side, her strawberry blonde curls damp with perspiration. "Sun's coming up," she whispers. She gives me a little hug.

I understand now something that Jenna, the Elder, had said, that a High Priestess' energy is so shiny that people in her coven fall in love with her—a good reason for not having married men in your coven. I have no sexual interest in my High Priestess, but I feel an outpouring of love for her. I feel very close to her, as close as I've ever felt to another woman.

I will never forget what she's done for me this night. I will never forget the look of pride on her face as I, her student, stood in that circle tonight. I will never forget that moment when she passed on that power of our lineage to me and that moment when I took my vows to God and Goddess and what I pledged. I still have that sacred feeling of my body as a living altar to Deity.

Though Donna says it is my right to say all that I experienced as an individual in my own rituals, I will not tell all, though I will tell bits of it over time, I'm sure. What happened tonight was between Spirit and me. It means nothing to anyone else. It would only be gibberish or mystery or something both pretty and strange, much like what Jan saw in her worrisome dream.

What happened tonight is between Spirit and me, and is for me alone. Not for Donna, not for the other participants, not for the other Third Degree candidates, not for Lady Dragon. This Elevation can only be given by Spirit and taken away only by Spirit.

"Did you find her?" I ask about Lady Dragon. I don't look in Donna's face. There's a nervousness in Donna's eyes now that I don't know how to contend with. It's easier not to look. I stare instead at the pale shades of sunlight in the East. I wish Leo were here instead of wherever he is.

I wish I knew where Leo disappeared to. I really could use one of his famous readings about now. He promised me a full-length reading as his Third Degree gift to me, and for weeks, I've been looking forward to hearing his advice on my impending divorce and on The Treat.

Not that I'm greedy for a gift. No, what I really want is a reading so I'll have some idea what to do about my Third Degree challenge. I've already convinced myself that Dragon Hart isn't quite a cult, at least not at this point, so if I leave, it won't be for that reason. But do I leave or do I stay?

A reading from Leo could certainly give insight. Maybe there's a reason he's unavailable. Maybe I have to make this decision without input from anyone else.

If I stay, will Donna really understand? She's tried to be fair and objective, leaving it up to me, but deep down, I know she'll be hurt if I stay, particularly after Lady Dragon's promise to strip the current Elders of their rank and Elevate her brown-nosing yes-men instead.   I still haven't seen enough to make me leave Dragon Hart for good.

I know I have this mission I've been given, but I don't know how or why or when. And I know the mission is the same as Lady Dragon was given. Does that mean she doesn't have the mission any longer? Did she willingly give it up? Or was it taken from her?

As we sit at a picnic table, I play with the end of my braided cords, which I have wrapped twice around my waist. The silver one was for my First Degree and Initiation ritual, a symbol of the Goddess, with knots in the cord at certain spaces so that I might cast a perfect circle with my cords if ever I should need a circle that's exactly nine feet or eighteen feet or however wide in radius. The gold cord represents the God, and was bestowed on me at my Second Degree Elevation, with the appropriate knots. The black cord, symbolic of my Third Degree, is new and fresh and still satiny. Not worn like the other two.

I've braided them, both for easier wear and to honor the Goddess Brigid, the Goddess of Light and Poetry and Fire and Healing who is known for Her braids and was Christianized as a saint. I feel safe inside my cords, a gentle reminder that when I wear them, I am not like other mortal men or women. I am most certainly a Child of the Gods.

"Did you get to talk to Lady Dragon about what you wanted to?" I ask again. I'm trying to be discreet in case Butterfly and her loose tongue are eavesdropping.

"No. I still haven't been able to catch up with her."

"You haven't been able to catch up with her? Or she hasn't granted you an audience?"

Wow.   I can't believe that came out of my mouth! Suddenly, I've gotten very blunt. It must be the lateness—or the earliness—of the hour. Or the lack of sleep. I'm not usually so daring in my statements.

A little gasp escapes from Donna's throat, almost as if she didn't mean for me to hear it. "Did I mention to you how proud of you I am? You think all these gifts you've been given recently are great, well, just wait until you start receiving the gifts of Spirit now that you have your Third. You're going to be amazed at—"

"You're changing the subject." I realize I'm no longer speaking to her as a student to a teacher or a neophyte to an Elder. I'm talking to her now as an equal. It feels strange...different.

"You're right." Donna sits up straight and lets out a long sigh. "Yes, Dragon's been avoiding me ever since we got here. She avoided my phone calls before we got here and I haven't been able to catch her alone since we stepped foot on the campground. She's always got Jeri and at least three other Third Degrees I don't really know well within a couple of feet of her. Geez, what's with this? It's like I can't have any time alone with an old friend. Like they're shielding her."

"She doesn't want to hear what you have to say." The words just pop out of my mouth. I don't know why. Just that it's true.

"She knows what I'm going to say. She's psychic. And even if she weren't, she's already asked that if I leave Dragon Hart voluntarily, that I tell her at this gathering and then it'll be official at Samhain. That'll give me time to say my goodbyes and make the transition to being on my own again. So why is she avoiding me? I've been trying to reach her for days. She knows I'm leaving. I'm positive of it."

The words start tumbling out again. "Yes, she knows you are leaving. But that's not why she's refusing to see you." I don't have any more information to give Donna.

"Jeri said Dragon's going to have breakfast with her new Elders-to-be in an hour or two. All of Dragon Hart is to meet at the Main Ritual site for a quick business meeting and then have breakfast."

I nod. Already, I can smell sausage links and hash browns burning as the newest Dedicants of Dragon Hart prepare the morning meal for the entire campsite. The business meeting is usually a list of announcements for the rest of the camping trip, followed by group singing, an introduction to the new Dedicants, then First, Second, and Third Degrees. There are always lots of Dedicants, sometimes nearly a hundred. Then there are fewer Firsts and even fewer Seconds, with the new Third Degrees from last night being among select few who have made it through the difficult training. The last thing that happens in a business meeting isn't so much business as an inspirational message from Lady Dragon herself, occasionally interspersed with tearful testimonials from various Third Degrees about how the God and Goddess have moved in their lives in the past year or what charities their covens back home have funded. At the end of the meeting, the number of the total membership is announced and Lady Dragon asks if anyone is moved to follow a different path, and that if they are, they may freely go. No one ever says a word. I know Belinda never had the chance when she left.

And although my Third Degree challenge is to decide whether to stay or go, I'm suddenly feeling more pressure to make a decision by the end of the business meeting. Or, if I do choose to go and if I don't want to stand before the whole group and feel like a blasphemer after a motivational speech from our spiritual leader, I need to talk with Lady Dragon soon. Very soon.

"I need to catch Dragon before that morning meeting," Donna says. "If I don't tell her before the meeting convenes, I'll have to announce my resignation publicly. I really *don't* want to do this publicly."

"She knows." There go the unbidden words again. "She knows it's hard for you to do this in front of the whole group. That's why the delays." The word *hu-miliation* pops into my head, but I don't say it. But it's there. It startles me. I feel a sense of joy at Donna's humiliation, only it isn't my joy. "You need to insist," I tell Donna, "that Lady Dragon sees you now. Right now."

Donna nods. "I'll go find her. I'll insist." Then she rolls her eyes. "If I can get through Jeri."

"You can get through Jeri. You've been an Elder for fifteen years. You're one of Dragon's oldest friends. You told me once that she's like a mother to you. You can walk right through Jeri if you want. The only reason Jeri has any authority at all is because Lady Dragon gives it to her to keep you at bay. That way, you won't tell your oldest and dearest friend that she's wrong to try to take so much power for herself. She can't face the challenge, so she's got her bodyguards around her to keep you from calling her down on anything she's done that's inappropriate. She knows you won't do it publicly, so she won't see you privately. But you can make the others leave. They *will* leave. They won't stand up to you. They draw their power from her. Or—" I have a strange thought—"she draws power from them."

"Okay." Donna thinks about it, then nods enthusiastically. "Okay. Yes. I'll go find Dragon right now. I...do you want to come with me? You can if you'd like."

I'm not sure why Donna asks. Maybe for moral support.

"You can tell her later—or whenever you want—whether you're leaving or staying. You don't have to decide yet."

"No, I'm coming with you."

I have no idea if I will say anything to Lady Dragon other than *Merry Meet* and *Blessed Be*. I suspect she knows I've been toying with this decision to leave. She is psychic, after all. So is Jeri. So are many of her new Elders-to-be. So are the Voudun Priests she's become more and more involved with in the last year.

I've had to shield heavily since Donna told me about my Third Degree challenge. There's been...stuff...around me. Energies. I've *felt* something at work for the past few days. Something I can't explain. Something meddling and close. I've felt it working to keep me close to Lady Dragon, but now I feel something tingling and warm on my shoulders like a mantel. Like the protective wings of crows around me.

The Morrigan. It's Deity I feel. An ecstatic rush of power around me, and I know I'm protected. I inhale and close my eyes.

"Ooooh. Did you feel that?" Donna coos beside me. "She's here. The Morrigan is here."

I keep my eyes closed. "I know."

Ten minutes later, the sun is already warm on the campground and we've located Lady Dragon inside Jeri's tent. Two of the Elders-to-be stand guard. Yes, *stand guard*. I've never seen this before. I'm used to seeing a handful of people around Lady Dragon, almost like they enjoy being in her charismatic glow and must follow her every footstep. This is different. Even though we've occasionally had trouble before at this campground with Boy Scout groups, local Baptist churches, and curiosity seekers, there's never been a need for bodyguards. At least a fifth of our membership have mundane careers in law enforcement or emergency services, so we always have plenty of campsite security to supplement the more doubtful security of the park rangers who always make it their mission to interrupt at least one ritual to see if we have drugs behind the sheet-curtained clearings. They never find any drugs, alcohol, or nudity. Our group is family-oriented, and I've personally found it more child-appropriate than the Baptist Church I grew up in. The park rangers always seem surprised...and disappointed.

"I'm here to see Dragon," Donna announces, marching up to the tent.

One of the guards crosses his arms. He's in his late 40's, a Southern Baptist preacher from Georgia, not far from where I grew up, but his congregation doesn't know he's also a High Priest of the Dark Goddess. I don't know his mundane name. He goes to great lengths to keep his Baptist identity a secret and never allows his photo to be taken at our gatherings.

The Southern Baptist preacher/High Priest of Wicca crosses his arms. "When Our Mother wishes to speak to you, she'll call you," he intones through his nose.

"What?" Donna pushes him aside. "Don't give me that shit! Dragon? Dragon, get out here, will you? I need to talk to you, and I need to talk to you now."

Someone hugs me from behind and spins me around into ample arms. "Raven!" It's Merewynn, another of the Elders. I haven't spent much time with her this year, and last year, she was sick with a migraine. She's thin, a little older than me but her face still unlined, and she doesn't color her flowing gray hair.

"Hi, Merewynn."

"I wish I could tell you what your energy sounds like. It's beautiful, sweetheart. Just beautiful."

Merewynn looks weary, as if gravity is her enemy. Like most of us, she's been up all night. Unlike most of us, she has some serious health problems. She's one Elder who will never leave on her own. She'll wait for Lady Dragon to strip her of her rank and then toss her aside. To her, unlike to me, Lady Dragon *is* Dragon Hart, the embodiment of the Mother Goddess Herself.

"I do hope, Raven, that you'll attend the workshop I'm teaching later today."

"Um, I...I don't know. I'll try."

If you're here, I hear in the back of my head.

"Are you teaching Tarot again, Merewynn? Because we really have to talk about that Tower Card." I try to make a joke of it, but it comes out sounding lame.

Merewynn, on the other hand, is somber. "No. Not at all. What we discovered last year when we polled all the Third Degree High Priests and Priestesses in Dragon Hart and every other coven I know of was that only about a tenth of us actually *see* energy. You know, like a purple flame or an electric blue flame when you cast a circle. Yet, it's one of those things that most people expect pagan clergy to be able to do. To *see* things. I mean, we're witches. We're supposed to *see*, right?"

I smile and think of Lisa, my student-to-be with the Gift of Knowing and the Gift of Healing, the one who often tells me she can see energy and has questioned why I am so inept as to not have these gifts.

Merewynn continues. "I mean, most of us can feel the energy, but very few of us see it. And I discovered five years ago that I don't see energy. I...*hear* it."

"Really?" Okay, this is interesting. I've heard of people hearing voices. I've heard of people hearing events. But hearing *energy*? Although I suppose a voice could be a pattern of energy.... This is new to me.

"And like tonight, Raven, all you Third Degree candidates in a circle? It was like a symphony. Each of you playing your own instrument. When you jumped into the circle, it sounded like a trumpet. But not a trumpet I've ever heard before. This was like an otherworldly trumpet. And Butterfly, she sounded like harp music, just fluttery and flittering all over the place. And Jonny, he sounded like a foghorn or a cross between that and, well, some kind of horn. Some of the instruments sound like ones I've heard before and some sound like—I don't know—instruments from other planets, other civilizations, lost cultures."

In the periphery of my vision, I see Lady Dragon emerge from her tent. Merewynn looks up and sees her, then quickly scurries off, obviously not knowing who was in the tent with Jeri.

"It's okay," Lady Dragon says to the preacher-Priest. She dismisses him with a wave of her hand. "I guess I'll have to talk to Donna now. All this time with me, and she has yet to learn patience."

Lady Dragon is not a physically imposing woman. She's in her mid-fifties, a bit frail, and looks nothing like the photos on her website. Her hair is thin and much of it gray. Her cheeks and arms are bony as though she's been without nourishing food for a long time or on the kind of strong medications than turn muscle stringy and weak. There's a sunken, hollow look to her that always shocks me when I see her. She has her long hair braided into knots down to her waist. Her long, tie-dyed T-shirt hangs almost to her knobby knees above her worn sandals. If the definition of a cult leader is someone who drips in diamonds and gold, then Lady Dragon is certainly not it.

She glances at Donna but barely acknowledges her. Instead, she lifts her gaze to me and gives me a slight nod, but it's more of an acknowledgement than her supposed best friend received. She turns back to my former High Priestess. "Donna, what is it you're bothering me about now?"

Lady Dragon says it in a joking manner, but it doesn't sound like a joke. She sounds…bothered. Something in her tone sounds familiar, and a snake of dread coils in my stomach. Jeri and the others stand a good ten feet away, forming a loose circle around Lady Dragon and Donna.

Donna looks annoyed. "Could I speak with you in private? It's fine if—" she waves a hand in my direction— "if Raven wants to listen, but this is really between me and you and it's…I don't know…it's…."

Lady Dragon shrugs. "You can speak in front of them. I don't mind."

"I-I do!"

Donna's stuttering. I've never heard Donna stutter before. She's one of the strongest people I've ever met, but her fear comes out in stutters. Right in front of my eyes, she is shape-shifting into something else. A child? A child who's frightened and knows she can never do anything better than screw up.

"Oh, *all right.* Jeri, you and the others go ahead and get my chair prepared for me at the business meeting. I'll be there in about five minutes."

Again, dismissing Donna. Cutting her short. After all their years of friendship.

Halfway through my Elevation, Lady Dragon had asked the candidates if we wanted to continue the Elevation or leave Dragon Hart. I'd answered truthfully to both questions. Yes, I'd wanted to continue the ritual. And no, I did not want to leave Dragon Hart. I *don't* want to leave Dragon Hart. If she'd asked, "Will you leave Dragon Hart?" and I'd known, I would also have answered truthfully. So it occurs to me that Lady Dragon is not the least bit concerned that I, as a brand new Third Degree, would ever consider leaving. That just doesn't happen.

Jeri, the preacher-Priest, and two others walk slowly in another direction, one of them glaring over her shoulder at Donna. I've never seen that kind of behavior within Dragon Hart. The four of them stand perhaps twenty feet away, which is closer to Lady Dragon and Donna than I am. Apparently, that's as much privacy as they're willing to give.

"Well?" Lady Dragon says to Donna. "Talk. I don't have a lot of time."

Donna glances at the foursome on the periphery and purses her lips. "This is a private conversation." She jerks her head in my direction. "Raven can hear. She knows what I'm about to tell you, but otherwise, it's a private conversation." She emphasizes *private* and stares back at the foursome.

Without looking up, Lady Dragon snaps her fingers and the foursome trot off to the primary ritual area.

"Well, Donna? Hurry it up! You can walk with me until I we get to the ritual area."

Lady Dragon's tone had not been nearly so harsh last night when twenty-plus Third Degree candidates had waited in a line by the edge of the woods to be called into *circle*. She walked with each one of us, talking with each one of us in a motherly way that had been sweet and wonderful.

When it had come my turn, she'd wrapped an arm around my shoulder and I'd been a little nervous at her touch, but I'd shielded well and I'm convinced that she didn't detect any doubts underneath my surface. She'd put her arm around me and told me she understood what a hell of a year I'd had and that I had gone through many changes and I had shed the old and was ready to start the new.

It was a beautiful, inspirational speech. Lady Dragon at her finest! At that moment, I understood what it was that had made her one of The Chosen Ones with a special mission from the Gods—to create an organization like Dragon Hart, to train others for the clergy, and to open doors that pagans alone would never have known existed, let alone that they were locked.

Last night, she'd been like the old version of Lady Dragon. The one who'd been explained to me as kind, loving, generous with her students. We'd reached the outer circle of the ritual area, and there I had seen hundreds of familiar faces that had gone on this path before me and had experienced for themselves the Elevation in a sacred communion with Spirit. Third Degrees, Elders. As well as my fellow candidates who'd been in line ahead of me, now waiting, watching, listening—as I was—to Lady Dragon's every word.

With the heel of her sandaled foot, Lady Dragon eked out a line in the dirt in front of me, barely visible in the light of the wide circle of torches around us. The line separated me from the circle where I was to be Elevated, to be reborn as a Third Degree High Priestess of Wicca in the Dragon Hart Tradition.

"There!" she said in a voice loud enough for everyone to hear. "You see that line? That line is the boundary between two worlds. What's on this side of the line represents your past and what's on the other side of the line represents your future. When you step over that line—if you choose to step over that line—you choose to leave all of this shit behind. Everything that's held you back. You leave it behind!"

I stared down at the line in the dirt, at her dirty heel, at my own feet. I'd already kicked off my shoes. I always prefer to be barefoot in ritual. I took a deep breath—and jumped over the line and into *circle!* With Lady Dragon at my back and my past behind me, symbolically at least, I felt the burdens start to ease. I was ready for a new life, ready for a rebirth, ready to start over. So ready!

And yet now, a few hours later, standing here in the woods and watching my spiritual leader, her hands on her hips as she talks with Donna, my former High Priestess, there's an odd prickling at my brow, almost as if my sixth chakra is opening up and I am seeing things with The Eyes of Spirit. I've been so worried that my Third Degree Elevation didn't "take" last night because I don't have that sense of euphoria that everyone's talked about.

And yet, I am suddenly seeing things I've never seen before. My High Priestess, right before my eyes, becomes not the strong woman, not the strong Elder I've known for several years, but a child or perhaps a battered wife. The way she holds her head, the way she lifts her gaze just enough to meet Lady Dragon's eyes. Her hunched posture, as if to say psychologically, "I'm no threat." I've seen dogs do the same, showing their Alpha dogs that they know their place in the pack, that they know their own lowly worth. I see that now in Donna, and it shocks me. It's like she's a different person. It's like she's....

She's *me*. I'm looking at *me*. I'm seeing what people have seen in *me* when I've been beaten down, when I've questioned my own worth. I see what Lisa saw and her friends saw the night of the Beltane party when I was with Quent—head bowed, worried, solicitous, down-trodden.

It's almost as if Donna is two women and this is a side of her I've never seen. It's weak. It hurts to watch.

"Well, spit it out," Lady Dragon tells Donna. "You've been pulling at my apron strings all week to speak to me. Well, here I am. You got me. Speak to me." Donna starts to say something, but Lady Dragon interrupts again. "Well? Spit it out." Donna opens her mouth and Lady Dragon silences her with, "Oh, Goddamn it, Donna! You're nothing but a weakling. Like I always say, a witch who can't kill can't cure."

Donna is flustered. I know how she feels. I've felt that way so often myself when Quent would berate me for…nothing. Suddenly, I'm not looking at Lady Dragon talking to her friend Donna or even her enemy Donna. I'm looking at Quent talking to me. The stance is the same. The words are the same. The tone is the same. It's not just Dragon or Quent but it's my father, too, with his harsh, cutting tone. And then it's every other manipulator and verbal abuser I've ever known.

I shake my head but it doesn't go away. Spirit is showing me something, something I don't want to see. It's like a curtain opening. No. A curtain rent in two. And I see what's behind it. The ugliness. I cringe. I can't help it.

"I've been thinking," Donna continues in a meek voice. "About, um, um, well, about—"

Dragon rolls her eyes. "Look, I've got to get to the primary ritual area for the business meeting. If you're not going to say what you've been pestering me for days to say, then fine. I'll—"

"No, I'll tell you. Wait. Wait. Dragon, wait! *Theresa!*" She uses Dragon's mundane name. I've heard it only once or twice. Donna's pleading but trying not to plead. Her voice cracks. She sticks her hands into her pockets. "Theresa, please. This is hard enough."

Dragon pats Donna on the shoulder. Three quick, short pats. Not particularly gentle. "That's why I think it's time we get some new blood in our Eldership. You know, Donna? Things just shouldn't be so hard."

Donna blinks several times and tries to collect her thoughts. "That's what I need to talk to you about... Dragon...Theresa."

I barely recognize Donna anymore. This is not the person who trained me. Not the person who's been my pillar of strength for the past three years. The dynamics between her and Dragon are the same as those between Quent and me. Donna and I may be super-strong women in any other situation and everyone else may see us as strong, but match us up head-to-head with our abusers and we become lost children again, pleading for a crumb of affection or respect.

"It's okay, Donna," Dragon says. "It's okay. I'm a gifted psychic, remember? I can see right through your weakness. You want to tell me that you're leaving, right?"

Donna bows her head and nods. She's shorter than Dragon, and she looks for all the world like a little girl who's been caught masturbating by her fundamentalist Christian grandmother and is being told she's going to hell.

Dragon presses a kiss into Donna's forehead. "Then I won't make you say it. You get your things and get off the property. You have five minutes to say goodbye to all your friends here, and then I want you gone or I'll have you arrested for harassing my group. Do you understand?"

Donna just stares at her as if to say, *But I'm not done!* Finally she finds her voice, and it's thin. "Raven...." She flails an arm in my direction. "Raven knew I was leaving. I told her it's up to her whether she wants to stay or to go or—"

Dragon shrugs and turns to me although she's still speaking to Donna. "No need for her to say anything. I already know what she's going to do."

I blink at her. "You do?" Maybe she *is* just that gifted because even with what I've just seen, I'm still not sure. I'm shielding as hard as I can, still feeling energies working around me to keep me tied to Dragon. However, the veils around her are dropping by the dozen.

"Of course, I know what you're going to do." She smiles broadly at me, smugly, taking a few steps so that Donna is to her back, cut off, alone. Psychology. Against Donna. Against me.

The Eyes of Spirit settle over me. Something flashes in the air in front of me. The dossier Dragon compiled on me, the one someone sent to my post office box with all the incriminating evidence on Dragon. Astrological charts. Illegible notes. Records of face-to-face meetings with various psychics within Dragon Hart to discuss me—but without the actual notes from the meetings. I catch the look in her eyes and hear her thoughts: *I have plans for you, little girl.*

Then it's all there! The last of the veils drops and I see clearly. I have struggled so hard for so many years to leave behind the verbal and emotional abuse I was raised in and later that I was married to. I have worked so hard to put it in my past and move forward into a new life. I have risked everything to get to this point in my life and start afresh, without the putdowns and the manipulation and the iron-fisted control. For as much as I honestly love Dragon Hart and the people in Dragon Hart, how can I ever stay here with a spiritual leader who possesses the abusive nature of the people I'm desperately leaving behind? How can I trade one master for another?

A strange sense of power comes over me, as if something just broke wide open. I squint into Dragon's eyes as she smiles at me. Everything feels as if the planet just halted temporarily on its axis.

"Spirit has just made it quite clear to me," I begin in a quiet voice, "that I am to leave Dragon Hart to— "

The words just tumble out before I can stop them. I have no idea what I'm saying until I hear the echo in my ears. An excitement rises in my chest. This is not a bad thing that I'm telling her. It's something wondrous. There's a mission that the Goddess has in mind for me. Plans She has for me. I feel wrapped in The Morrigan's dark-winged embrace.

I try to tell Dragon what it is but she stops me. She throws up a hand and interrupts even before the smile has a chance to fade from her face.

"Well, fine!" she shrieks at me, flinging up her hand in dismissal. She doesn't want to hear my reasons. She's heard enough. Anger rolls off her in a hot wave, pushing invisibly at me. She pivots on one foot and stalks away, her graying braids dancing against her hips. Over her shoulder, she screeches, "Have a nice life!"

I stand, numb, staring after her, suddenly aware of the dozens of my Dragon Hart family who stand motionless in the park, watching, eyes wide, unsure of what just happened. Everyone seems as afraid to move as deer aware of the smell of hunters.

Dragon's words hang in the air. *"Have a nice life!"*

"Thank you," I whisper, without moving, without breathing. "I will."

I've answered my challenge. My Elevation is now complete. And the most incredible sense of euphoria fills every cell of my body.

8

Sunday - New Moon in Leo, Waxing

I have never been so glad as I am tonight for my feet to touch the ground. I have a thing for earth as an element. There's something about it that calms me, grounds me—literally. I read somewhere that if we're missing a particular element in our astrological charts, then we're likely to have an affinity for it. We crave it, just as I crave having my feet in the grass to calm me down or to energize me. The fondness for the missing element adds balance, and in my chart, I have virtually no earth and very little fire.

I'm a Pisces girl. Triple Pisces with lots and lots of air, almost exclusively in Aquarius. I guess that means I have lots of great ideas but, as a Pisces, I feel them very deeply.

The fire I have is mainly in Uranus, which relates back to the fire of my spirit and my fury for change and transformation. But earth? Almost none. Just in Pluto. Nothing much to ground me. So my heart is always on my sleeve and my head in the air.

But since my divorce and now since my Third Degree, I'm becoming more and more okay with that. It's not that there's anything wrong with me. It's just the way I'm wired, and I would neither change it nor medicate it for anything in the world.

I'm driving home from the airport now, 10:00 on a Sunday night with my lone suitcase in the backseat of my black Mercedes. I'm glad now that I didn't drag all that camping equipment to Maryland and back to Florida. It's been a long day, given the threats of Hurricane Charley and not knowing whether my plane would make it back to Florida.

But it's been a long day, too, because of what's happened over the weekend. I had paid to camp for the whole weekend. I had paid for all of my meals and yet, I'd been forced to leave early or face being escorted out by both park rangers and Dragon Hart's security squad. That had meant I would have to sleep in a hotel and pay out even more money here in the midst of my divorce when I don't have money to pay out for spare expenses—and thankfully my airfare to the Grand Coven meeting was paid for months ago. Fortunately, Barbara offered Donna and me the guestrooms in her house.

Leo never came to say goodbye, but Tyler had, smelling strongly of dragon's blood, his signature scent. I was sure when I'd hugged Tyler goodbye that, yes, he was the one who'd sent the package anonymously to my post office box. He couldn't or wouldn't leave Dragon Hart entirely—maybe because he feared losing Leo—but he'd done what he could to warn me.

I'd not been able to change my flight for a later flight home. Even if the airlines had been accommodating, the hurricanes had seen to it that I could not yet return home.

As I turn into my driveway, I'm bone-weary. I've already called the girls from my layover in Atlanta and they're to be home and waiting for me. They're old enough to be alone for a few hours, so there's no problem there. Quent was to have dropped them off at the house at 7:00 and they were to have worked on their homework and gotten ready for me to come home. Yes, they could have been sent to bed, but I know they won't stay there and they won't sleep. They'll want to see me and know I'm back. Both are too frightened I might die and they'll be sent to live with their father permanently. I'm sure they'll be awake, and I have missed them so much. I'd wanted to take them with me on this trip, but I couldn't, and now in hindsight, it was good that I didn't.

Quent's car is sitting in the driveway. My stomach knots up. *What's he doing here?* Yet, for the twist of nerves in my stomach, there's something different about this. It's...power. It's anger and it's power. Armed with the energy of my newly Elevated Third Degree, I feel powerful, bright, shiny, like nothing can stop me. I like this feeling. A lot. I've put up with so much crap from him, and now he can't touch me. I'm strong, and I'm much stronger than he is. He doesn't know who he's messing with here. He's messing with a Child of the Goddess!

I exit the car and pause for just a second at the outdoor altar I've set up at the willow tree. It's a simple pile of stones. A stranger or someone who didn't know better might think a pet had been buried there. They are beautiful, flat stones acquired from mountain creeks. Some, the girls picked out for me.

The rock on the top, the Coven Stone, is one that the Elders of Dragon Hart blessed for me a year ago as a way of tying me back to the Grand Coven when I was physically so far away. It's an odd-shaped rock from the State Park where Dragon Hart meets every year. If I use my imagination really hard, I can see five points to the rock, like a pentagonal star is built inside it. As I stand before it, it zings with energy as though it recognizes me. I touch the braided cords under my T-shirt—wrapped around me three times and well-hidden—and I feel safe.

I am not like other mortals. The affirmation repeated at my Initiation and Elevations rings in my mind.

I open the door and pass the Main Altar. Like the Coven Stone, it pulsates in greeting, recognizing me as I enter the foyer of my home. The altar is an old library table that Quent's mom threw out and then two months after she *gave* it to me, she discovered that it was actually an antique, worth several thousand dollars. She's never failed to remind me of this.

Over the past three or four years, I've done a lot of magickal work at this table. It's definitely been infused with energies. I've done spells here for protection, for healing. Rituals that included facing the South and calling upon the Archangel Michael to wield his mighty sword and cleave truth from deception in the case of Quent. I have prayed at this altar many times but tonight, after the girls go to bed and certainly after Quent is gone, will be the first time as a Third Degree. I'll plan a gratitude spell....

No. Maybe it's better if I do a protection ritual first. Dragon is angry, so angry that I could *feel* her all the way home from Maryland. And though I have wards of protection in the house, I've never had any against members of my own coven.

"Mommy!"

I hear both girls squeal as they realize I'm home, then the patter of bare feet on the floor as they round the corner in pajamas and then throw their arms around me. They feel wonderful to hug. I've missed them so much.

"Wow," Rhiannon whispers in my ear. "Mommy, you're vibrating."

Sonnet nods into my chest. "You're warm all over. Like really hot. Like a fire."

Quentin joins us in the foyer and lays a hand on each girl's shoulder and proceeds to rub as if he's claiming them for himself. Both girls simultaneously shrug off his grip and hug me harder. They've spent two school nights and a weekend with their dad, and it's probably more time than he's spent with them in the past two years. The judge says the minimum time he can spend with them is every Wednesday night for three hours and every other weekend. He complains that it's not enough, that he's an equal parent, and yet it's more time than he realizes, more of their daily lives than he's used to. Equal parenting sounds good in theory and it's important to his image, but in real life it doesn't work that way. It never has. Not with us.

"Girls," he instructs, "why don't you go to your mother's car and get her bags out for her. Give us a chance to talk."

The girls don't let go of me. He purses his lips. I can feel the dark energy all around him. The weird-ass diet he's been on for the past two years, the one he's tried to impose on the rest of the family, has left him emaciated, his eyes sunken, and he's lost most of his hair. I get a good look at him now, both in the physical and in the spiritual sense, and I understand why Rhiannon asks over and over, "Mommy, what did you ever see in Daddy? How could you have ended up with him?"

He looks like walking death. There's a sense of cancer or something dark all around him, eating away at him. Hepatitis crosses my mind. AIDS crosses my mind. Something's wrong with him physically, and for as often as I've begged him to talk to Dr. Matthews about it, he's blown me off or outright refused. He tells me there's nothing wrong with him, yet he weighs less than I do. Friends and acquaintances who haven't seen him in several months often call and ask me what he's dying of or if he's terminally ill. They try to ask it in a gentle way, but they're clearly concerned. To him, though, he's perfectly healthy—physically, emotionally, spiritually—and it's the rest of us who are ill.

"Girls!" he says in a stern voice that makes all three of us shudder. "I said, go get your mother's bags out of her car."

The girls sigh and huff, then race out to the car to make the chore as quick as possible.

"How was your trip?" he asks, as careful as ever to make polite conversation. Polite conversation is important. It has to do with image.

"The trip was fine."

I give him no more, no less. The previous two years when I'd called him from the camping trip at the Grand Coven meeting, he'd been light and airy whenever he'd talked about how things were at home, but the second I mentioned how things were going in Maryland or something about a workshop I'd attended on "Historical Astrology: Fixed Stars in the Middle Ages," he'd immediately clammed up, sullen, punishing me for being gone, for defying him. If we didn't talk about my Grand Coven meetings, then none of it existed. Except that I always felt like I didn't exist when he gave me the silent treatment.

He smiles through gritted teeth and makes an earnest attempt to be pleasant. "I'm glad you had a good time. We made out here okay without you. The girls were very good. Maybe if you and I are able to work things out and get back together, then maybe I could attend your next camping trip with you."

Yeah. Right. After all the times I've begged him? Now, when he thinks it's the right thing to say to get back into my life, he's willing?

"There won't be any more camping trips to Maryland. I've left Dragon Hart."

He jerks his head up and grins. This time, it's genuine. "Really? You left? You've given up the whole witchcraft pretense?"

"No," I answer firmly, "I've left Dragon Hart."

"But...but why?"

He's still happy. I can hear it in his voice. In a way, he blamed my spirituality for my decision to not be married to him anymore. He was right. Without my spirituality and without the training I had in Dragon Hart, I never would have had the courage or the insights to leave him.

"I'm still a witch," I tell him, "whether you like it or not." His smile fades just a little. "And I'm still Wiccan. As a matter of fact, I'm now a Third Degree High Priestess of Wicca. Again, whether you like it or not." His smile fades a little more. "But I have left Dragon Hart. I'm no longer a part of the organization."

He shrugs. "Wh-why? All this time that you've been with them. Why leave them now?"

"Plain and simple? I looked at Dragon and realized that she was a verbal and emotional abuser. Like you are."

His gaze shifts downward but only for a split second. He doesn't deny it.

"Well." His tone is patronizing. "I know that that was very hard for you and I know it took a lot of courage for you to stand up to somebody like Lady Dragon."

I'm not sure if he means it or not, but I shake my head. "Actually, it was a lot easier than I thought it would be. You, Quent. You were the one who was hard to leave. After you, everything else has been a cakewalk."

All he can do is blink. Then he gathers himself and leans against the door to keep the girls out. "We need to talk about finances."

Yes. Of course. Finances. He moved out around the first day of August, refusing right up until then, even with my lawyer getting a court order from the judge to have him thrown out at midnight. He'd barely made the deadline and only then with his computer under one arm and a couple of changes of clothes under the other. He'd planned to come back. He was sure that I wouldn't go through with the divorce. He still is. And with every attempt of his to control my life and to keep me in a marriage I don't want to be in, I've become more and more sure that the divorce will happen and that I will never back down now.

"There's a problem with our joint account," he says.

The joint account we've had for sixteen years. For the first two years, we'd kept separate accounts and a household account that we paid expenses out of, and we'd each put in 50% of the needed cash, even though his income was two-thirds of our combined income and I never had much of anything left over in those days. He'd insisted we combine the accounts. Not that he thought it was unfair that I put in the larger percentage of my salary but because he didn't think it showed the proper amount of my trust in him by keeping a separate checking account. He was determined to have our money put together. I didn't understand why then, but I am slowly coming to realize that we have lived off my salary for years, and I have no idea what he did with his.

"What's wrong with our joint account?" I ask. "I told you that I was no longer paying anything out of the joint account and that I've opened a new account at another bank. You said you were going to do the same."

"Lauren, I haven't started a separate account yet. I'll do that later." Meaning he hopes I'll withdraw from the divorce before he has to change accounts. "And I know you have a separate account, too, but you need to put that money back into our account."

I blink at him. "What money?"

"The money you took out of our joint checking account. I've already paid my security deposits and my first month's rent. That was $6000 right there."

I swallow. Six *thousand* dollars? That was first and last month's rent and a small security deposit on one of the priciest apartments in town. He made a huge deal of not moving out of the house until he had no choice, then he'd made a big deal of not having a place stay though he hadn't looked. Even though his mother had offered her empty basement apartment for a few months—for free. And his brother had offered his spare bedroom for a few months—for free. And his other brother had offered his second house for a few months—for free. And his sister had offered her grown-and-gone daughter's bedroom for a few months—for free. All within five miles of our house. He insisted it was incredibly difficult and extremely expensive to find any place he could rent on a month-to-month basis. He refused to rent any place longer than the minimum allowed, which was two months. He wanted to drive home the point that a physical separation, however temporary, would cost *money,* and *money* was important.

His mother, on the other hand, had been magnanimous enough to recommend he stay in our house with the girls and *I* could stay in her basement apartment while she "worked" on me and helped me see the error of my foolish ways so he and I could work things out. I'd seen how she had sidled up next to Quent's sister's estranged husband, wormed his secrets and fears out of him, and then used them against him. There was no way in hell I was going to let her do the same to me or leave my kids home alone with Quent while he's online making arrangements with his $300-an-hour escorts.

"Anyway," Quent tells me, "there's no money left in our joint checking account. And your lawyer contacted mine about paying child support? The amount he quoted was absolutely ridiculous."

"The amount my lawyer quoted to yours, Quent, was based on your income. There's a formula for the State of Florida. It's based on your salary and my salary and our joint income for the past year."

His face darkens. "I don't have the money to pay that! I don't know where you think I'd get that kind of money. You already emptied out our joint account—"

"No. No, I didn't empty anything. I opened a new account with the paycheck I got after you moved out. And

I've paid several big utility bills you neglected to pay during the summer so I could continue services. I didn't take half of the money out of our joint account even though I was entitled to it. I left every penny in there, including my full paycheck from two weeks ago which was far more than was required of me. So if you've overspent it—"

"I haven't overspent anything! *I'm* not the one who spends money like crazy. I've been going to a counselor. That's what you *wanted*, isn't it? For me to get *counseling?* Well, I've been going to a counselor and I've told him what's been going on between us."

Clearly this isn't the Methodist minister he's speaking of. The minister had told him to get his *arse* out of the house and give me some time to work through the trauma and heal. That was the last time he'd seen the minister for counseling. He switched over to a therapist his employer pays for and I'm not sure what Quent's told him, but I have a feeling he's left out some pertinent facts.

"My therapist says there's nothing wrong with me. It's all *your* problem. I'm tired of being the bad guy here, you know? I'm not a bad person. I am *fine*. I've looked at all my issues in the past couple of weeks and I am *fine*. I'm *fine!* I'm emotionally healthy! And if there's anything wrong with anybody, it's *you!* You just need to grow up and forget about all this spirituality crap you keep spouting and these…these shitty little books you want to write that aren't worth a hill of beans and get back to concentrating on your *real* career. You know, if you'd concentrated harder on your career over all these years, you would've been bringing in a better salary and we'd have a better lifestyle than we do. Instead, you're just trying to kick me out on the street!"

The veins in his forehead bulge. His cheeks are red…purple…darkening. What's in his eyes is…hatred.

"Lauren, if we're able to work things out, I'll tell you one thing: things are going to change between us. It's *not* going to be like it has been."

I start to agree, but he cuts me off.

"We'll get to do things that *I* want to do for a change. You'll stop talking about witchcraft in public and stop writing about it and stop embarrassing me in front of my friends with it. You know, I didn't even tell my parents and my sister where you were these past few days and why I got *stuck* watching the girls. I told them you'd gone to a writers' conference because at least then it was legitimate. There was no way I was going to tell them you were with your...your...*cult!* How much exactly did that trip cost? That money should have been in our joint account!"

I don't remind him of his last tour of strip clubs across Canada with his gay friends or the $3000 hotel bill I'd spotted before it had vanished. Instead, I speak with a calm that I don't quite understand. "My trip was paid for months ago with money that was a personal gift to me." From the Elders.

"Well...well...." He grits his teeth and shakes his head. He reminds me of a bulldog. "You just need to concentrate on business and grow up and stop playing around like you are and take life more seriously. You only live once." Before I can say anything, he adds, "And I don't want to hear any more of that reincarnation shit. You need to focus harder on making a living and having the kind of life that we want."

"We?"

"Yeah. *We*. Instead of us being broke all the time. It's all about you, Lauren. You, you, *you!* You want to quit work and stay home with the girls while you write your silly little books, your worthless books. You're still mad at me for that, aren't you? You know we can't afford it."

I'm boiling inside. And yet I don't show it at all. I let it pass through me and over me. I remind myself for only a moment that no, we couldn't afford for me to stay home with the girls and have my dreams of writing full-time, yet we'd paid more in taxes for each of the last two years than I'd grossed at a day job I found profoundly un-fulfilling and often spent ninety ours a week trudging through. Quent readily paid for anything his gay buddies from high school wanted, often keeping it from me until one of them accidentally mentioned a new computer or expensive gifts while I was in the room. Yet, we never had the money for me to follow my dreams, even though I en-visioned a richer, happier home life for us all. We could live the life that only he imagined.

"You know," he says, "I've been thinking. I think we can get back together and we can work this out. I know I said I wasn't going to contest the divorce but I've changed my mind. I *am* going to contest it. I'm going to contest it on the grounds that our marriage is not irrecon-cilable because *I believe* we can get back together and *I believe* that we can make it as a couple."

His sunken eyes are bulging now. He's yelling. But I'm not cringing. I'm still okay, I'm still okay, I'm still okay.

"But Lauren, things are going to change. Things are most certainly going to change. And *you're* the one who's going to do the changing!" He pulls the door open and almost falls over the kids with my luggage and then stomps off to his car. A few seconds later, he squeals out of the driveway while I'm still standing here, watching, dumb-founded.

"Mommy?" the girls are saying, hugging me. "Mommy, it's okay. Mommy, don't be upset."

I'm trying not to show it, but I am upset. Quent couldn't hold it together long enough to try to cajole me into borrowing money from Jan just to refurbish the bank account he's depleted on God-knows-what. I'm trying to be calm, I'm okay, I'm okay, but the girls seem so worried about me. They won't stop hugging me.

Then I realize that the air is coming out of my lungs in a wheezing sound. Sonnet runs to get me a glass of ice water.

I didn't mean to, but I let him get to me, just that quickly. It isn't as bad as usual and standing up to him was easy. I'll thank my Third Degree Elevation for that, but Third Degree or not, I can't change overnight what's been a part of my life for over twenty-three years. I can't stop cringing at the sight of him simply because I got my Third Degree a few days ago. It's too ingrained, like the indention on my ring finger where I used to wear my wedding band. It's been months since I've worn it but the indention is so deep that it looks as though I took the band off only minutes ago. This history with Quent is a part of me, whether I like it or not, and it won't fade overnight and it won't fade easily.

Even if Leo swears that a new man is going to be popping into my life any day now.

Gods. Right now, I don't want to be around any man at all. I just want to be left alone. I just want to be free. I just want to be by myself. I'm raw and I'm wounded and I need time to heal.

Gods, send me a healer. I send my silent prayer into the night air as I stand between my front door and my altar. *And when I do fall in love again, make him a man with integrity who'll love me exactly as I am, a man who'll "get" my writing and understand my spiritual nature and be my emotional support and let me be his.*

I let Quent throw me off balance. Damn it. I did. I tried not to. I didn't mean to. I was calm in front of him, but on the inside, I'm nothing but Jello.

Sonnet hugs me even harder. She's my little empath. She can feel the things I feel. It's been that way with her for several years now. I knew it that first night she huddled in her bed, crying in pain because of what she felt, and what she felt was how I felt the night Quent was so angry he'd locked me out of our bedroom. I'd slept in bed with her, which wasn't that unusual, given that she's prone to nightmares. But on that night, while I'd semi-slept, she had curled up next to me, shaking all over, so tied into my third chakra that she knew every vibration I felt, no matter how I tried to hide it.

Sonnet is the one who said to me, even when she was a tiny girl, "Mommy, why is that when you're smiling and everyone else thinks you're happy, I'm the only one who knows how sad you really are?" She and I were connected that way. We always have been. Since her birth.

"Mommy," Rhiannon tries to soothe me. "Come sit down. We've got some pillows on the floor in the family room and they're prepared just for you so you can get comfy and tell us all about your trip."

Rhiannon isn't an empath, but she is an intuitive. She does know what's going on. Probably far better than anyone realizes.

The family room looks exactly the way it did when Quent lived here. He hasn't picked up the furniture yet. So far, he's refused to. He tells me there's nothing in the house that has any sentimental value, including all the furniture that was a personal gift from me. There's one ironic exception to his blanket refusal: he's suddenly become very attached to his mother's old library table in the foyer, the table I use as my Main Altar and where I've done most of my magickal work for the past seven years.

The family room is in the process of being reborn. It's the room that the girls renamed a year ago as the "TV Room" because there was no "family" to it anymore. Instead, this room is where Quent spent twelve hours a day on the weekends, watching episode after episode of some old comedy or detective show he'd recorded on TiVo, refusing to go anywhere with the girls and me as a family and, at the same time, angry if we went anywhere without him. The rest of us ended up tiptoeing around the house and trying not to disturb him while he watched TV show after TV show after TV show after TV show. He'd bought a new TV, bigger and better than ever before to go with the TiVo recording system and had expanded our cable subscription to include digital TV and 900-plus channels.

The girls had merely shaken their heads and asked why we needed so many TV channels. They knew all the time that they would get with him would be in front of the TV with him. The rest of the time he would spend supposedly at work or on the basketball court with his male friends. He replaced his multiple hours per day of porn addiction with TV and let me know constantly what a terrible sacrifice it was but that he was, after all, at home and not doing anything wrong. Physically, he might have been home, but emotionally? He'd never been farther away.

I sit on the pillows with the girls and think about how I want to change this room. I want to make it different, make it mine. I want to get rid of this furniture that reeks of nothing but TV-watching. I want to throw it all out.

But that assumes, of course, that I will go through with the divorce. I'm pretty sure now that I will. I know, I know. My friends think I'm stupid for having second thoughts, but I've invested so much into this marriage. And the hope that Quent really will change is so seductive. Shiny. A glimmer. The times when things were good between us, it was really good. At least, I think they were. But those had been only crumbs and I'm still waiting for the feast. The sadness I have is not for what we once had but for what was never there, no matter how much I wanted it to be or how much I tried to make it be there. If he doesn't come back, if I do go through with the divorce, then I want to get rid of all this old furniture that belonged to his mother. It will have to go back to her. I never wanted it. She just needed a place store her unwanted old furniture and somehow it became ours and then I couldn't get rid of it or replace it or send it back or give it away or throw it away. Because it belonged to his mom and she didn't want it back and we didn't have room for furniture that was any nicer. It wasn't antique. It was just junk that she was too sentimental about to get rid of when she got new furniture and my house was big enough to store it in. It wasn't my style, wasn't my taste, wasn't me. Hell, it wasn't even Quent.

If I have a chance to re-do this room, I'll do it in greens for growth and purple for spirituality, and I'll have walls that have color to them. None of this brown-carpet-white-wall crap Quent had insisted on year after year after year. Something in this house will finally reflect *me*. But first, first I should re-do the master bedroom. If I go through with the divorce, that is.

I recline on the floor pillows with the girls and I tell them all about my trip, every last detail. They cheer when I tell them how I left Dragon. They want to touch the cords around my waist, under my T-shirt. They tell me they feel the vibrations off from the cords and the glow from me. I still can't quite calm down after the confrontation with Quent, but I give the girls hugs and slip off to bed anyway. I'll get some sleep and then tomorrow, I'll do some protection rituals against both Dragon and Quent.

Quent slept in my bed last night and let the girls sleep in their beds. He didn't have my permission to be back in the house, but he took advantage of the situation. Nothing new there. I don't want to sleep in the bed after him. His energy is still there. I'll purge it tomorrow but for now, I'll sleep in one of the twin beds I've pushed together in the guest room. The girls crawl in beside me.

They fall asleep first, the rhythm of their breathing gentle and steady. Soothing.

Home. I'm home. I've started my new life. I'm still in the glow of my Third Degree. Life will be good now. I know that Donna has said that your Third Degree is a series of Second and Third Degree moments, little trials to get you on track and teach you things and then moments of great joy and freedom and connection to Deity. At the moment, I just feel really good and I want to feel really good and I like feeling really good. It's been a long time since I've felt good.

I close my eyes and open them, close my eyes and open them. Close my eyes and open….

There's something in the room with me.

The girls sprawl at my back, Sonnet pressed close against my spine and Rhiannon flailed against the wall where the twin beds have been pushed together and into the corner of the room. This is the room that feels good, the one where the fairies live. We feed them every day from a little bowl of milk. Ever since we invited them into the house at Solstice last winter, we've offered them food and shelter.

It's strange what happens with the milk. Under normal circumstances, it would sour within a given number of days, but when fed to the fairies, left out for their energies to feed off, strange things happen with the milk. It doesn't smell or stink up the room. Yet, when the negativity in the house is worst, the energy in this room is still good, and this is the best-feeling place in the entire house, then the milk instead turns hard as a rock and sits in the glass. It turns hard fast. *Within hours.* It doesn't sour over a period of days. It's as if all the nutrients and energies are sucked out of it almost immediately. The more negativity in the house, the faster it happens. Sometimes, when Quent lived here, the milk was changed twice a day.

The thing that's in the room with me now is not a fairy and it's not *of* the fairies. I can feel it. It's not that light, flitty, fairy energy. This is different. Dark. Ominous. I see it forming in front of me, across the room as I lie with my cheek against the pillow, eyes open, watching it.

I'm not asleep. I have not yet slept.

It forms in profile. Stylized. A metallic, silvery gray. Its outlined curls coil this way and that. Somehow it looks Transylvanian to me. It's Old World. Romanian?

Maybe Germanic. Definitely not Celtic…or Egyptian…or Norse…or Greek…. I've never seen anything quite like it, but out of dark vapor, it takes shape. Solid. Metallic.

From where I lie in my bed, I see its head and chest. I hold my breath. I don't move. I'm not asleep, and this is real.

It's a *dragon*. A metallic, silver-gray, Transylvanian dragon sitting in profile in front of me, its eyes looking straight out, jaws open, teeth sharp, steamy drool dripping over the dark gums.

Its eyes angle straight toward the North, then its gaze cuts toward me, toward the West, and it sees me in my bed. It says nothing, but I know its purpose. Its purpose is to scare me to death. Anything short of that would be failure.

But still I don't move. I know what it is. I know *who* it is. It's Dragon.

Lady Dragon, I hear her correct me.

I've heard about this. I've heard from Donna and the other Elders about how Dragon learned to use astral projection to visit her students, usually coming to them to let them know to contact her in the days before email and cell phones were so popular. It's a conscious ability she has, and while it started as a way of getting messages to her loved ones, I've also heard that she's used this to frighten people when she's angry.

It didn't make sense to me before. I couldn't imagine it before. But now it…*she*…stands in front of me, a dragon preparing to eat me alive!

I should have done a protection ritual. I should have made preparations. I should have finished warding the house. But I'd been too tired, too off-balance from my confrontation with Quent.

Help me, Gods, I think to myself. *Help me, Lord Herne, Cernunnos.* I'm not sure why I call on Him instead of the Goddess, but it feels right. *Herne, Great Hunter, protect me.*

I call upon the God, something I haven't done so very often since I left Christianity seven years ago. I rarely called upon Him in my First Degree, though a little more in my Second Degree when I immersed myself in those energies. I haven't thought as much about Him as I need to. Calling on Him now comes instinctively, but He is not the God of my Baptist childhood. This is something much more primal.

I cannot move. My body has turned to lead. No matter how hard I try, I cannot lift even my head from my pillow. All I can do is lie here, poisoned and paralyzed and just watch as the dragon turns, razor-sharp teeth, acid-hot drool seeping from the gums, eyes gleaming with anger and betrayal.

Help me, Herne! The words do not even escape my throat. The best I can do is think them. I haven't even the strength of my own to raise my voice to my Gods to save me.

I feel the breath of the dragon on my bare feet, peeking out from under the edge of the covers. I feel the weight of it in the floor as it crosses the room toward me, the joints of its legs bending deliberately, heavily, moving forward, mouth leaning in close, teeth above my throat.

Help me, Herne!

A black vapor forms between the dragon and me and swirls around, taking form. A stag! Mighty and angry and boasting antlers like I've never seen on this plane!

I blink. Herne. It's Herne, my God.

He lowers His head to make sure the dragon can see the sharp points of His antlers, but all she does is snarl back at Him, blowing steam through her nostrils. He is not amused. He shakes the mighty rack on His head and then lunges, skewering the dragon in the throat. He pulls back and lunges again, this time in the heart. Blood seeps and covers her. She does not die. She merely fades to curls of smoke…and is gone. The Stag looks over her shoulder, back to me, scarlet dripping from His antlers. He lowers His head and gives it a little nod as if to acknowledge me, to let me know that He is here if I should ever need Him. And then He, too, is gone.

"Mommy!" Rhiannon screams for me. Suddenly I can move. I flail myself into the other direction, rolling over in bed and reaching across my sleeping Sonnet to shake Rhiannon awake, but she's already awake, awake and staring wide-eyed at the ceiling, terror still painted on her face.

"Are you okay?" I whisper. I'm calmer than I expect to be.

She hesitates, then nods and cuddles closer to Sonnet and me. "I had a bad dream," she tells me.

"It's okay. It's all gone now."

She shakes her head frantically. "No, it's...it's still here. It was awful."

"Do you want to tell me about it?" Sometimes a little catharsis is good for the dreamer.

Rhiannon snuggles closer. She curls in against my arm, drawing it to her and holding on. "There was this thing," she says. "It started at my feet." Her voice trembles. "It was eating me alive!"

"It's okay, sweetheart."

"It was big and mean and metal, and it had these really sharp teeth. It was eating me!" Her gaze locks with mine. "It was some kind of animal, like a wolf or a...a—" her eyes widen—"a dragon."

Damn it. Damn her!

I bolt upright out of bed and head toward my Main Altar while Rhiannon snuggles next to her little sister. It's one thing to mess with me, but to mess with my kids? No! Dragon has met Rhiannon once at the Grand Coven meeting I took her to last year. She knew Rhiannon, and there were no problems identifying my daughter. They'd met on the physical plane and a connection had been made, so

Dragon could reach her on the astral. Sonnet, on the other hand, was safe. They'd never met. Dragon could establish that connection only through me, and I now visualize my protective shields around my baby.

I lean against the Main Altar, relish its solidity. I should have warded before going to bed. I should not have let Quent throw me off balance. I can't take it back, but I can stop it now.

I grab a pen and small square of note paper, then draw a pentagram on it. In the middle of the pentagram, I write Dragon's names, both the magickal name and the mundane name. I put the names I know of her cronies, her bodyguards, the ones she was drawing energy from. I write the name, too, of the two Voodoo Priests she's become associated with. There's something about this magick she's using that feels different from the energies of The Morrigan and Herne. Dark, like They are dark, but dark in a different way. A different flavor of dark.

My stomach twists in knots. I pull my cords tighter around me. *I am not like other mortals....*

I place a picture atop the altar, face up. It's a ceramic tile, actually, of The Morrigan. A beautiful Celtic piece of artwork given to me by a Dragon Hart Initiate as a thank-you for playing the part of the Western Gate at her Initiation. On top of it, I place the square of names on the paper, and on top of that, a mirror, face down. It's a simple ward, but it's been effective in the past. I invoke The Morrigan and Herne to watch over me and mine, over my house and over my family and to protect this property and keep it safe from all intrusion but especially from the intrusion of Dragon and her ilk.

That ecstatic connection with Deity tingles down my spine once again and I feel the mantle around me like a giant raven's wings folded over me and around my house like a shield. I feel something pinging off it. Dragon. Still trying to get through to me. But my shields are up. She can't get through now. I won't let her. By the power of The Morrigan and Herne, I won't let her.

I tiptoe through the house quietly so I won't wake the girls, the two of them cuddled into the warm spot I've left behind. I open a dresser drawer and begin pulling out things. I extract my wedding album and ignore the photos of Quent and me in happier times. One picture strikes at me. Cheeks red because I'd cried throughout the ceremony for some unknown reason.

I flip past and find a photo of Granddaddy and me, him in his best Sunday suit and me in my wedding dress. He'd been in his seventies then and quite dapper. I pull the photo from the plastic insert. It sticks for a second and then releases to me.

I open another album, one of the girls. I find a photo of him holding Rhiannon when she was two weeks old, a proud smile on his face but looking much older than in the wedding photo with me.

And then I find one last photo of him, this time holding Sonnet on his lap. He was old and weak and feeble and only months from dying when this picture was taken. Sonnet had been two years old at most. My mom had held her discreetly on his lap while I snapped the photo. He hadn't been able to hold her. He'd been through two major heart attacks, the funerals of two wives, and a lifetime of hard work. He'd wanted to hold her but hadn't had the strength in his body any longer. He'd fretted to me while I took that picture that Rhiannon was five and might remember something of him, but this baby was too young. Sonnet would never remember him, he'd said. His voice had cracked.

Now I gather all three pictures and take them back to the Main Altar. I arrange them on the altar, close to the front door, close to my threshold where nothing can pass.

"Granddaddy," I say. "Alva. I know you've been here ever since Quent moved out. I've felt you in my home from the minute he left and sometimes even before. You're welcome to stay. You're very welcome to stay. But I need your help now. I need you to keep this place safe for my girls and me. Both from Quent and from...other things."

I feel his presence. Between the altar and the front door. It's like a force field.

I sit on the floor across from the altar, legs crossed, arms folded, back against the wall, and try not to see Dragon. When I wake, the sun is streaming through the door, landing on the pictures of Granddaddy and the girls. The mirror is still face-down, anything that Dragon and her cronies might do reflected back to The Morrigan. I have her trapped there, yet I still feel her pinging at my shields like pebbles thrown against the window.

I want to call Donna, but it's too early. Donna and the Elders need to know what happened last night, and I need their help. I can still feel Dragon striking at the wards around the house. What if she gets through again? I can handle it if she sends a dragon after me. At least I think I can.

But what if she messes with my girls? They'll have to get up again and go to school. What if she harangues them there and gives them waking nightmares in the middle of class? Sonnet seems to be fine, given that there's absolutely no connection between Dragon and her. Sonnet seems to sense something going on outside the house, but it's much like feeling a storm rock the shingles when you never get wet. Rhiannon, on the other hand, is still whimpering in her sleep.

I wake both girls anyway and send them on to school. No choice. I'd be remiss as a mother otherwise. I'd love to have them home with me today, safe and sound, but instead, I have to put a bubble of protection around them and send them out into the world and ask the Dark Mother to keep a watch over my babies while I can't.

As soon as the girls have left for school, I know I need to shoot a quick email to Belinda, telling her what's happened. She needs to know. There could be repercussions for her as well, especially if Dragon thinks that I've left Dragon Hart to follow Belinda's footsteps. Yet, when I sit in front of the blank computer screen in my home office, I have no idea what to say. I've always been told that you don't talk about Dragon Hart business to anyone who isn't part of the group. But Belinda was a part of the group. She was the one who introduced me to Dragon Hart.

Oddly enough, I have a message from Belinda waiting in my inbox.

```
DID YOU MEET "THE TREAT"
AT THE GRAND COVEN MEETING?

I KNOW LEO SAID YOU WERE
GOING    TO    BE    MEETING    HIM
SOON.

I JUST WONDERED IF YOU FOUND
HIM.
```

I smile. I've kept her up to date on my divorce and the prognostications of the future man in my life who will share a grand mission with me. She'd thought that maybe I'd find The Treat within Dragon Hart or at least through the group, though she'd had no psychic insights that he'd be a member of Dragon Hart. Just that I'd meet him the week of the Grand Coven Meeting.

```
BELINDA,

I'VE LEFT DRAGON HART.
```

That's all I type before I hit send.

She's online, and a message comes back immediately.

TELL ME EVERYTHING.

I FELT A DISTURBANCE IN THE
FORCE!

Belinda and I really never talk by phone because of our schedules, so I spend the next two hours composing my email to her, telling her about the past couple of years within the group. I tell Belinda how I saw Dragon's abusiveness. I tell her all about the cult checklist. I tell her about the visitations from the astral dragon and how it tried to eat Rhiannon in her dreams. I tell Belinda everything I can jam into the email and then quickly hit SEND as the phone is ringing.

It's Donna. I know it is, even before I pick up. That's different. I'm definitely more tuned in since my Elevation.

"Hello, you new High Priestess, you!" Donna chimes before I can press the handset to my ear. Her perkiness fades as I tell her the events of the evening. "I'll call you right back," she says without explanation.

I sit and wait for almost an hour, occasionally rising to water a plant or dust a table. I keep my cords wrapped tightly around me. *I am not like other mortals....*

When Donna calls back, there's a cacophony of other voices and noises in the background. "Hey, I brought reinforcements," Donna informs me. "Sorry about the delay. We had to conference you in."

"Hey, darling!"

"Hey, sweetness!"

"Hi, Raven!"

I recognize several voices among the other Elders. Barbara, Mariah, DeeDee, Jenna, Beverly.

"How are you feeling?" Barbara asks. I can't miss the motherly affection in her voice.

"Frankly," I say, "I'm pissed—"

"No. No, no, no. That's not good. If you're angry, that's exactly what she wants. She prefers abject terror, but anger will feed her, too. She wants to get an emotion out of you." Donna had definitely filled them in on everything.

"Well, she's doing it. Of course, she's getting an emotion out of me—she's messing with my kids."

"You can't do that, Raven. You can't let her get that kind of emotion out of you. She feeds off of it. She feeds off of fear and anger. You show either, and you're giving her your strength."

"I refuse to be afraid of Dragon, even if, down deep, maybe I am a little bit. I want to think that she can't hurt me, but the things I've seen? Maybe she can. She can certainly scare my children."

Barbara clears her throat. "It's best if you just laugh at her."

Barbara's been gone from the Grand Coven longer than any of the other Elders. She hadn't wanted to leave. She'd been forced out early by Dragon for challenging Dragon in a personal confrontation that had little or nothing to do with the Grand Coven. Mariah had told me it was because of the way Belinda had left Dragon Hart and how coldly Dragon had treated Belinda because Belinda had felt pulled by Spirit in a different direction.

"She doesn't have the power to hurt you," Barbara says, "unless you give her the power. There's nothing she can do to you." The other Elders echo their agreement.

We talk for another hour until it's time for the Elders to leave for their different jobs. I've already told my boss that I won't be at work today and that I need an extra day to recuperate from my spiritual retreat. It's a good thing now. They'd probably think I look pretty silly wearing a suit with my Priestess cords braided and swinging from my waist. Eventually, I'll have to take them off and hang them up, but I'm not ready to yet.

I'm not like other mortals....

I pace around the house. I'm restless, nervous. I haven't slept well. I'm focusing all my energy on the shields around the house and around the girls. I'm tired, so tired. Half-way out to the mailbox, the phone rings. I grab the mail and run back inside, thinking it's Donna again.

"What's wrong?" Jan asks before I can even say hello.

"Oh...I'm sorry. I forgot to call or email and let you know I was back."

"I knew you were back. I could feel it. Now I want to know what's wrong. I don't know what the hell is going on, but I do know that I don't appreciate this Dragon-Person of yours showing up in *my* house in the middle of the night."

"She what?"

Jan isn't mad at me even though she sounds like it. I know Jan well enough to know that she's on her own version of the warring Mother Goddess. Barely into her sixties, she's old enough to be motherly toward me, and her claws are out when she's protecting her young. Right now, she's thinking of me as her young.

"That bitch showed up in my dreams last night," Jan says. "Only, I wasn't dreaming. I was wide awake."

"She came to you as a...as a...dragon?"

"A what? No. As a woman. Younger than I thought, though. Early twenties. Long blonde hair."

"That's not Dragon." Then I remember. At a workshop at a Grand Coven meeting a couple of years ago, Dragon had talked about using different astral forms, both as an animal and as a woman. One of her favorites was a young Valkyrie with long blonde hair.

"I don't know what she looks like, Lauren, but I know what she looked like last night when she walked into my bedroom out of thin air, and that was definitely your Dragon."

"What happened?" I'm almost afraid to ask.

I flip through the mail in my hands, mostly bills. I open a few, particularly the ones marked PAST DUE. My bills are always paid on time. There's a bill for lawn service, one that Quent always pays himself because he personally knows the company's owner. I've given him the check to hand-deliver so he can do his glad-handing in person...except that the past four months of lawn care haven't been paid for. Quent insisted on using this particular company, even though they're horribly expensive, rather than buying a mower and doing it himself. They were a good customer of the bank where he works, and he'd said it was important to make a good impression on them. I wonder, looking at a past due bill of nearly $1,000, what kind of impression has he made now?

"This Dragon-Person," Jan continues. "She showed up in my room while Hubby was sleeping next to me. I was lying in my bed. I wasn't asleep. You know how I get when I'm contemplating a new painting."

I nod into the phone, even though she doesn't see me. Jan doesn't live by the clock but rather, by the paintbrush. She paints some on this canvas and then sleeps for however long she needs to and then wakes up to paint some on another canvas. So being awake at 4:00 in the morning is nothing unique for her.

"What time was this?" I ask.

"Three thirty-three. Magic number, huh? Anyway, she showed up in my bedroom. Lauren? That bitch threatened me."

"She what? She doesn't even know you. She's never met you. She knows about you...because Donna had to give her your address so my Third Degree exam could be mailed to your house instead of risking sending it to my house where Quent might have gotten hold of it. So she knows I have a friend or a...oh. You know, I think Jeri, one of the new Elders-to-be, thinks I have a sister named Jan."

"Yeah. That's it. I feel it. That's right."

I smile. Ah, yes, an empath and a psychic for a best friend. There's nothing I can hide from Jan and little that others can hide from her either.

"Anyway, Lauren, I told that bitch to get out of my bedroom and get out of it right then and not to ever come back on my property and that she has absolutely no authority over me or mine."

"And what happened?"

"She got this rancid look on her face and left. Just faded away and then she was gone. But I'm still pissed. I've been up all night pissed about this and all morning, too. I debated over whether I should call and tell you. I tried to call earlier but the phone was busy."

"I'm really glad you did, Jan. I'm sorry I didn't call earlier to fill you in, but things didn't go so well last night with Quent." I take a few minutes to explain.

"You need to be extra careful of him," she warns. I know she has her psychic hat on at the moment. "He is up to something and no matter how sweet he might be here and there, it's all a façade."

"I know, Jan. I do. I'm not getting back together with him. Don't worry."

"Well, good, because I'm worried about what he might talk you into. I know it's very seductive that you have this hope that he really will change. But you know he's not going to."

"I know, Jan."

"No matter how much you might want him to."

"I know." She seems to be worrying more than usual. I flip through the rest of the day's mail and stop at an envelope from the mortgage company. I rip it open and pull out the contents.

"You okay?" Jan asks. I've been silent for a few seconds.

"Yeah. It's just—" My eyes are stinging. I wipe away a single tear. "I just got the paperwork on our mortgage where we paid it off a couple of months ago right before the divorce."

Quent had alleged I'd waited until the house was paid for before I divorced him. One had nothing to do with the other, yet the house has always been special to me. It represents both the good and the bad, my hopes and dreams. It's a bigger house than I ever wanted, far showier, but Quent had wanted it, then had insisted on the brown carpets, blank white walls, and nothing that seemed vaguely related to my personality inside it, including me. Over the years, I've made it mine, but every time I talked about my dream of staying home with the girls, he told me we couldn't afford it because we lived in this nice house. I would have been happy in our little dollhouse on the other side of town but finally, with some good investments, we'd been able to pay off the house. He'd promised that once we paid it off, I could stay home with the girls and write my heart out. That never happened.

"You okay, Lauren?"

I sniff. "Fine."

"Okay, so you'll have to buy out his half of the house, however much that is and of course with the current market like it is, that's going to be twice what you paid for it, but I think you're going to get to keep the house. I know to you this feels like the Tower card in the Tarot deck, but it's going to be good, sweetie. You just need to get your self-confidence back. You're going to be able to afford so much more than you ever thought you could."

"I-I don't know about that. I guess I'm just going to have to wait and see."

"And I hope, too," she says, "that you are thanking your lucky stars that you did not refinance that house like he wanted you to."

It's not just my lucky stars I have to thank, but Jan, too. Before she became a famous artist, she'd been a real estate lawyer. When Quent came home with roses and a sudden financial plan for our future and my intuition had screamed that something was wrong, Jan was the one I'd gone to for advice.

The value of the house had gone up—way up—and suddenly a $200,000 home was worth well over half a million. He'd wanted to refinance the house, even though we'd owed only $20,000 on it at that time. He'd suggested we refinance the full value at an adjustable rate that would only go up. When I'd said no, he'd been livid.

No matter what numbers he presented to me, none of it made sense. He couldn't make it make sense. He'd said it would save money in the long run, but I couldn't understand how taking out a loan at a higher rate than we already had and for the full value of the house could possibly be better than paying off the last $20,000 and being done with a house payment forever. Tax-wise, we needed the deduction, but psychologically, it felt good not to owe anything.

Granted, he'd reminded me that he was the banker in the family and that he knew about these things and I didn't. When I mentioned it to Jan, her face had turned purple. As a real estate lawyer, she'd seen this ruse a number of times. The husband would convince his wife to refinance the house for the full amount, he'd take the equity out of the house and hide it in the Caymans, then he'd divorce her and leave her with the house note—for the full amount of the house—and say he'd lost the equity while gambling in Biloxi so there was no record of its disappearance. It's clear now that the man I considered my partner in life had planned to do the same to me.

"Lauren, hang on…I've got a call coming through from my publicist and I'm going to have to take it, but you listen, Lauren: don't you let that Dragon-Person make your life miserable. She shows up at your house again? You tell her to get out of there and that she has no authority over you."

I smile. "Yes, ma'am."

Maybe if combine her advice and the advice from Barbara, Donna, and the other Elders, I won't have to concentrate so hard on keeping my shields up and strong. Maybe if I simply tell Dragon to get the hell out of my house and laugh at her at the same time, then she'll run and cower like the little dragon she is.

I smile again. I'm feeling better, much better. I can fight her. I can fight this. The only thing is, I resent that I even have to think about fighting her in this…this witch war that's started. I shouldn't have to think about things at all. I should instead be luxuriating in the glow of my new Third Degree. That and the fact that my ex has moved out and I've been reborn and I'm starting over and I'm doing okay. Not to mention the prospect of some guy known as The Treat on his way into my life soon.

This should be one of the happiest times in my life, at least for the next thirty days or however long you're allowed to feel the glow of your Third Degree. The last thing I should have to contend with now is a witch war with a control freak, egomaniac, verbal abuser.

I ignore the rest of the mail I retrieved while on the phone with Jan. It's mostly bills anyway.

I return to the computer to see if Belinda has responded, but first, I log onto the Yahoo email group I share with Butterfly and so many of the other members of Dragon Hart. It's not an official list. Dragon doesn't permit official lists. She doesn't permit unofficial ones either but as long we don't discuss our lessons or Dragon Hart business and keep our messages strictly social, the email

group is permitted. In hindsight, I see that it's a control issue.

I wait for the page of new messages to appear.
Twenty messages scroll down the screen, each declaring
"I'm home" or "Congratulations on your Third Degree."
None of them are directed at me. But then, people are still
trickling in from the days-long drive.

Quickly, I type in a message saying hello, and that I
arrived home safely in spite of the hurricanes, and congratulations. I refresh the screen and my message pops up
immediately. I wait for a response but not one comes.
Butterfly and a name I don't recognize continue to post
messages but neither answers me.

A message from Tyler pops up next, so I quickly
send a message back to say I'm glad he arrived home safely.
I ask how Leo's doing. My message doesn't go through.
Instead, the screen suddenly changes. I blink at the words.

NOT A MEMBER OF THIS GROUP.

I don't understand. I resend the message and get
the same response. I send it a third time.

NOT A MEMBER OF THIS GROUP.

Deciding to try again later, I switch to a list where I
can see the names of the members, but I'm not permitted
to look. I'm denied access. I don't understand. No one's
answering me and I'm suddenly not a member of the social
email loop any longer.

Confused, I shift screens to check email. Belinda
has responded but in an email not nearly so long as mine.
She tells me finally the whole story of what happened in
the last few months she was part of Dragon Hart.

She writes about the hurt of having the Grand
Coven shun her when she left and how she'd tried so hard

and so many times to explain to Dragon that she felt compelled to start her own spiritual organization, particularly a sister organization. That it was the call of Spirit and not her own preference. She didn't know why but she knew she had to, and she could not argue with the Goddess. Dragon had told Belinda she agreed: Belinda couldn't argue with the Goddess but she couldn't stay a part of Dragon Hart and she'd better be damned sure she knew if it was the Goddess luring her away or ego. Belinda had been "damned sure."

After her departure, Belinda, too, had had visitations from the metallic dragon. So had her children. Every last one of them. She'd erected shields, bouncing back the energy through the use of mirrors exactly as Dragon had taught.

```
IT'S A GAME WITH DRAGON.
A GAME OF PING PONG.

SHE SENDS THE ENERGY OF FEAR
TO YOU AND IF YOU HAVE YOUR
SHIELDS UP, IT DOESN'T COME
THROUGH.

YOU BOUNCE IT BACK TO HER AS
LONG AS YOUR SHIELDS ARE UP.
THEN SHE WITH HER SHIELDS UP
BOUNCES IT BACK TO YOU.

IT GOES ON AND ON LIKE THAT
UNTIL ONE OF YOU GROWS TIRED
AND YOUR SHIELDS SLIP.

AND LET ME TELL YOU, IT'S
NOT DRAGON WHO GETS TIRED.
```

SHE GETS OFF ON THIS.

YOU HAVE OTHER THINGS TO DO
WITH YOUR LIFE AND YOU WON'T
BE ABLE TO KEEP YOUR SHIELDS
UP.

EVENTUALLY SHE _WILL_ GET
THROUGH.

I start to email back and tell her what Jan had said about telling the blonde Valkyries to get the hell out of her bedroom. I could tell her what the Elders said about laughing, show her pity or amusement and watch the dragon turn its tail and run. Not that they claimed any personal experience with it, but that's what they've advised. Then I read the last line of Belinda's email.

MY FRIEND, MY DEAR SISTER,

PLEASE UNDERSTAND THAT

FOR A YEAR AND A DAY

AFTER I LEFT DRAGON HART,

MY LIFE WAS SHEER HELL.

9

September 2004, almost a month later
Monday - New Moon in Virgo, Waxing

Physical therapy hurts like hell, but I'm determined to make the most of every moment, especially these fucking leg presses. One way or another, I will get back up off my knees, metaphysically and physically. It's been four weeks since my Third Degree Elevation and the power boost from Spirit has been a huge help.

After six or seven months of warning my boss that eventually I'd have to spend some time in physical therapy and that I had not taken time off for sick leave when they were busiest, I reminded them throughout the month of August that I was taking all of September—the least busiest time for my current office—to take care of my knees. By the end of August, particularly after I'd returned from the Grand Coven meeting, my knees had suddenly gotten so bad again that I could barely walk at all. I hadn't had a choice but to take time off for my own health.

Even so, an hour before I was to leave work for medical treatment, when tears streamed down my face as I tried to walk from my desk to the photocopier, my new supervisor had given me a hard time because the former supervisor had approved my leave but the new one had not. Worse, every employee in my office had either quit or been reassigned elsewhere, leaving me as the only one to do the job. Even though they'd known about my planned medical leave for months, they'd done nothing about it. So when I announced I was leaving for five weeks of physical therapy, they'd railed against me for leaving them in a lurch.

Before my...rebirth...I would have cancelled my physical therapy and somehow hobbled to work, even though I was almost to the point of crawling. It took twenty minutes to walk up the steps—sideways—into my building, and that just wasn't acceptable. Even walking from my desk to the bathroom and back took thirty minutes of little baby steps. I was on my last leg, so to speak, and I literally could not stand anymore.

I'd waved a signed leave slip in front of my supervisor, showing him that my leave had been approved many months in advance. They tried to guilt me into staying but I refused. For once in my life, I was starting to take care of myself instead of everyone else, and I'd done it without feeling the least bit guilty.

My plan had been to spend the whole month of September writing book proposals for the new career I craved, but I'm well into the third week of September and I still haven't written a single page. My divorce has become a full-time job just to come up with the necessary paperwork to fight Quent.

He's done everything possible to slow-roll the divorce proceedings, thinking that every minute he delays me is another minute he can talk me out of it. The minute my lawyer asked for certain paperwork, Quent became angry and distraught again. I think he's still surprised that I'm going through with the divorce.

In retaliation, he's insisted on certain paperwork from me, including every transaction I've made for the last three years. He wants names, dates, addresses, lists of people I've sold my books to. He wants to interview my editors and publishers from over the years to see if they're holding back any money from foreign editions. He knows the money isn't there, but he also knows that the paperwork exercise will burn my time, incur more legal fees, and leave me angry. It's yet another way of manipulating and controlling.

The physical therapy is good for working out my agitation. I slam my legs hard against the weight of the leg press, shoving outward for the last ten times. In less than three weeks, I've worked my way up to 140 pounds. My knees are no longer swollen, or at least not as badly.

Cindie, my perky physical therapist, praises me to the high heavens for my progress. I've gone from being scared to death of even standing on the treadmill to being able to walk 2.5 mph. I'm still not able to take stairs well and I can go up them a little easier than I can come down, but I'm working on it. It hurts. Every day hurts. Three sessions a week for a hour and a half each, with ice and electrical stimulation to keep down the swelling.

"I'm worried," Cindie tells me as I finish the last leg extension. "We're just not able to drive out all the swelling. I'm still concerned about that. You have too much pain in your knees right now."

I'm not like the other students she has at the same appointment time. In particular, a college girl stops her exercises the minute Cindie leaves the room, and the girl thinks it's funny. She doesn't realize that she's cheating herself. She refuses to do anything that might hurt, even a little. But me, I take it on eagerly and get a little stronger each time.

Cindie bites her lip. I figure it's bad news. "I really think you might want to ask your doctor for some anti-inflammatories."

"Don't want them," I say. "I'm not a big fan of pills. The physical therapy is doing me more good than anything else right now."

"True," Cindie admits thoughtfully. She's about my age, dresses mostly in athletic shorts and tank tops, and bares all the long, lean muscles of a track star. "Still, have you asked your doctor? I don't understand why he didn't offer them to you."

"He did. And I refused them. I told him I preferred for pain to be my guide so I don't overdo it, and he said okay, that that's the way it should be."

"But you're still in pain. That part's not improving. Who was your doctor again?"

"Matthews," I answer.

Her receptionist, Ginger, snorts from across the room. She's young, maybe mid-twenties, married with a couple of children, and the opposite of Cindie. Ginger always has a frown on her face, even when she's happy.

"That's funny," I tease. "He says such nice things about you guys. He's the one who recommended your office to me." Actually, he'd recommended Cindie. Dr. Matthews had never said a word about Ginger. It wasn't just a matter of convenience, though Dr. Matthews' clinic is only two doors down from the physical therapy office.

"There he goes now," Ginger says, nodding toward the plate glass windows behind me.

I turn my head and see the tail lights of his Porsche.

"Leaving early as usual." Ginger grates out her complaint. "And speeding as usual." She lowers her voice. "Jerk."

Cindie shushes her, then says nothing else.

"Don't shush me. You know I can't stand him."

I'm dying to ask why not, but something tells me not to.

"Ginger!"

"I said, don't shush me!" Ginger mouths back something and straightens some files on her desk. She glances at her watch as she does every day at almost 5 p.m., which is the time I'm done with my session and about the time they close. "I'd love to see him stay here past five just once."

"He comes back," Cindie argues. "He goes to a fast food place for dinner and to be alone, and then comes back and works until the wee hours of the morning. He doesn't have to be here at five to leave when you do."

Ginger narrows her eyes to squints. "*I've* never seen him here after hours—"

I almost laugh. I doubt Ginger's ever been in the office after hours.

"Cut him some slack," Cindie says. "Dr. Matthews is having a rough time right now."

I wait expectantly, hoping for an explanation. I take my time gathering my belongings.

Ginger finally shrugs and turns to me. "He told Cindie once that he loves chocolate fudge. So I made some one day and brought it into the clinic to him and took it down to his office. I was just trying to be sociable."

Cindie laughs. "You and Roy were separated at the time. You were trying to more than being sociable."

Ginger shrugs again. "Anyway, he wouldn't eat a bite of it. Not a single bite. Said chocolate makes him hyper and asked me to take it away."

The thought of it tickles me and I laugh. "Hyper? As bouncy as he is? How would anyone know?"

Cindie laughs with me, but Ginger is still sullen in that spurned lover kind of way that seems to drift around her now. She presses her lips together and squints. She doesn't aim the hateful look at me. She'd never do that to a patient.

But something clicks in my mind. Ginger made a play for the doctor. While she was separated. *And he's happily married.*

"What he needs is a keeper," Ginger persists. She finishes cleaning up her desk area and fumbles with her purse, just waiting for the clock's hand to jump to the 12. "It's probably a good thing that things happened like they did with his wife. If you ask me, the last thing that man needs is children."

"So Lauren," Cindie changes the subject quickly, "are you planning to evacuate?"

"Evacuate? For what?"

"The hurricane. Ivan. It's supposed to hit here on Wednesday. Within forty-eight hours, they said. I heard somewhere that it's going to be a Cat 5."

Ginger snorts again. "This is—what?—the third or fourth hurricane within a month? Feels like somebody's trying to wipe Florida off the map this year."

Wipe Florida off the map. Oh, Gods. Not quite a month ago, Mariah had said something about how Dragon manifests things. She hasn't been able to get through my shields in the past month. Is she trying to bring other things in that can get through my shields? Including a deadly hurricane? She does rituals, according to Mariah. Ones that sometimes ask that her enemies simply have her wrath visited upon them. Sometimes, it's in the form of thunderstorms. Sometimes fires. Almost always by working with natural phenomena.

"What's wrong?" Cindie asks. "You just went pale as a sheet."

I suck in my breath. "I have to get home. Now."

Ten minutes later, I'm in my car and on my way home. Somehow, whether he was speeding or not, I catch up with Dr. Matthews' Porsche as he exits a gas station. I wave at him, but he doesn't see me. He seems distracted. There's a sadness all around him. I can tell it in the way he holds his head. I wonder what Ginger meant about his wife and children.

We sit at the red light, waiting, our cars side by side. For a second, he looks up and I think he sees me, but he doesn't. He looks right past me. A dozen crows light on the traffic light in front of us and on the wires leading to it. He looks up at them and smiles. Then the smile fades, the light changes, and he zooms off ahead of me.

What would he have to be so sad about? I wonder. He's a good-looking guy, early thirties, pleasant personality, seems to get along with almost everybody. Ginger being, to my knowledge, the only exception.

He's a physician, so he's got to be bringing in some big bucks. More than I am, anyway. He drives a cute little Porsche. He's married to a drop-dead gorgeous woman. He has a couple of kids. At least, I thought so until what Ginger said. I've heard on several occasions that his wife was pregnant, but I don't know for sure and I've never seen photos in his office. Nor has he ever spoken of his children, which is odd. He's the kind of man who would revel in his kids, and I've seen how good he is with my girls as well as with other young patients. The building he works in is known as the Matthews Building and several buildings nearby are owned by the Matthews Family, so to be so young, he must be doing well for himself.

And yet, the last few times I've seen him, he's seemed so sad, even when he's been friendly. Then again, I suppose, so have I. To the outside world, it would have appeared, for the last few years, that I had everything I could ever want. I wonder what it is that could make a man like Dr. Matthews so unhappy when he, too, seems to have so much. He doesn't show it, but I suddenly see something in him that startles me. He is alone in the world. For all of his smiles and jokes and light-hearted manner, he is as wounded as I am. And I have no idea why. I have a feeling I'll find out, though, when the time is right.

When I arrive at the house a few minutes later, the sun is low in the sky. Both girls are home from school. And I'm glad. They give me the usual hugs, ask about my knees and about my appointment, and tell me what they did during the day, all while I check The Weather Channel to see about this new storm on the horizon.

Sonnet presses her hand against her stomach, precisely against her third chakra, and I know she's feeling ill as she watches the TV screen. "It's not coming this way, is it, Mommy?"

My poor kids hate storms. We were trapped several years ago in our car, on an interstate and in the worst storm I've ever seen in my life. Sonnet cried and screamed and wet her pants through the whole thing.

"I don't know, sweetie," I say, "but it's a powerhouse. If it comes this way, we'll head up to Grandma's."

She seems to take in my words but then stares off into space. "No, Mommy, it's coming here. We better leave tonight." It feels right, what she's saying. In my gut, it feels right. "It's that Dragon woman, isn't it? She's making it come here."

I suck in a deep breath but don't answer. I don't want to lie to my own daughter. As the Elders told me, Dragon does have a way of manifesting things. And we've had far too many hurricanes this year criss-crossing the State of Florida as if to X it off the map. We don't live near the water so I'm not really worried about flood damage. But winds? At 160 m.p.h, will the winds leave anything standing?

I need a new roof, but we can't afford it right now. Quent hasn't paid child support for either August or September. And I've spent every penny of my after-tax salary to pay bills Quent didn't pay over the summer. Not to mention buying the kids clothes for school and property tax and car insurance. Expenses are mounting up and all my assets have been frozen except for my salary. I've already had to borrow grocery money from Jan. Meanwhile,

Quent lives in the nicest furnished apartment in town and his mommy cooks for him twice a day. We can't possibly have another hurricane right now. My schedule simply won't allow another crisis at the moment, and I'm far too stressed to even think about it.

"Mommy," Sonnet asks, "isn't there anything else we can do to keep that Dragon woman from bothering us and sending the storm to get us?"

Anything else we can do? Aw, sheesh, little one.

Sonnet, of course, has no idea how much I have been doing. Keeping my shields up. Feeling nightly for Dragon's pings against my force field. People who don't believe in psychic attacks have never had that kind of crap to deal with, and certainly never felt the silent writhing of energy in the Ether like maggots. It's easy to say it doesn't exist when it hasn't been in your frame of reference. Though I didn't *not* believe in it, I didn't have a real appreciation for it until I upset Dragon. She's settled down in the past few days, at least. But now I know why—she's manifesting storms.

I've known for the past month now, since the time someone—most likely Tyler—sent me that package about Dragon's underhanded dealings. She's very afraid of a U.S. tax audit and she's in trouble with the I.R.S. I've already paid a visit to the internet and gone online to the I.R.S. site to download their forms on penalties of tax fraud. I made copies and posted them strategically around the house near the entrances and thresholds. If Dragon wanted to astral in, she'd see those and know that I know her secret. It must have worked. Within a few hours of posting those photocopies around the house, the pinging had stopped and I felt her recede. Donna and the Elders had gotten a kick out of my tactics. But now, if Dragon is indeed manifesting storms, she is fighting back with something bigger than the I.R.S.—Mother Nature.

"Rhiannon," I say, turning to my other daughter who is busily flipping through TV channels in search of other news on the hurricane, "go to my altar supply trunk and get some things for me, please. A very small black candle, a very small red candle, and a very small white candle. Bring them to the kitchen."

While she's gone, I bend down to the floor, knees popping all the way down, and stand on my knees in front of Sonnet. "Sweetheart, I want you to listen. I'm going to give you a shielding technique, okay?"

"Will it work around Daddy?"

I laugh. "Yeah, it will work around anybody. Daddy, Dragon, anyone."

"Great. What do I do?"

"Okay, I want you to think of a flower. You love roses, right?" She nods. "All right, I want you to think of the biggest, most beautiful crimson red rose you can imagine. Got it?"

She closes her eyes. "Got it."

"Okay, well, that great big beautiful rose? That's you, sweetheart. That's everything about you that makes you *you*. Everything that makes you special and beautiful. Okay?" She nods. "Now I want you to imagine that rose blossom folding up into a really tight rosebud. Can you see that as it folds up really, really, really tight?" She nods again and scrunches up her eyes as she does. "Now is that rosebud still the same thing as that flower?" She nods again. "It's still just as beautiful and still has all that beauty and all that specialness in it, right, that the open rose blossom had?" She nods again. "Except that now it's held in really close and tight. You know all that specialness is still there. It just can't be seen or touched by anyone else at the moment, right?"

She nods. "Right."

"So whenever you're around someone who makes you feel upset and tense, you just imagine that great big rose blossom of yours closing up into a really tight bud. You're still just as special on the inside and just as beautiful as always, but you're holding that in very close where that person cannot touch. Got it?"

She shakes her head yes, grins, and opens her eyes, blinking. "Got it, Mommy!"

"Will these do?" Rhiannon asks as she returns with three candles.

They're exactly what I wanted. And just the right size—about as big around as my middle finger and just a bit longer. Being a working mom who's unable to sit at home by a candle for hours on end, I prefer the small candles because I like for my spell candles to, well, burn *out* during the course of a spell.

I send Sonnet after a baking pan, and she brings back her favorite cookie sheet for making her chocolate chip specialties. I place it on the countertop, safely away from any papers or other fire hazards. I dress the three candles with dragon's blood. It's one of my favorite oils. Ironically, it has nothing to do with Lady Dragon or Dragon Hart. It's a power booster for my spells and has that rich aromatic texture you'd find at a Roman Catholic altar loaded with myrrh and frankincense.

With a lighter, I melt a little wax on the bottom of each candle and stand them straight up on the cookie sheet from left to right: black, red, white.

"What's the spell for?" Rhiannon asks as I pick up a box of Celtic sea salt.

"Transmutation. We're going to *transmute* some energy. A very cool witch named Dorothy Morrison mentioned it in a workshop of hers that I attended." I smile at the memory. Dorothy and a popular Neo-Wiccan author, Slither Serpent, had co-hosted a seminar at a little pagan shop that was a good three hours' drive away. Dorothy had been well worth the drive and the sneering from Quent when I'd insisted on going and going alone, while Lord Slither had seemed a little too interested in a girl sporting a Kali tattoo.

"Who's Dorothy Morrison?" Sonnet pipes up.

"She's written a lot of books about witchcraft and magick, and she's fascinating to listen to. Anyway, I've modified the basic spell to suit my own needs, so this is really just a small part of it, but once you know how the whole thing works, you can take any part of what she teaches and tailor it to your own needs. For example, I don't remember what color candles she recommended, but since these three colors are important to Dragon—and she's the one interfering and sending negative energy—they have a directly symbolic reason for being used."

"But what's it for?" Sonnet joins me at my elbow and echoes Rhiannon's interest. "What's transmogrification?"

I laugh. Her sister's been reading old comic books to her. *"Transmutation.* It's a spell to shift energy from one form to another, and it can be used for any purpose. In this case, my intent is…."

Both girls look over my shoulder as I write the words on a piece of paper:

To shield me and mine

from the storm

"What's the salt for?" Sonnet asks.

I pour a thick trail of Celtic sea salt from the black candle on the left to the red candle in the middle. "Negative energy is being directed our way," I explain. "Although energy really isn't negative itself. Energy is just energy. But there's an intent that's been associated with this, and that intent is negative." I don't have to explain whose intent it is. The girls know.

"As the three candles burn, the negative energy will move from the black candle where it comes in and follow the trail of salt to the red candle. The red candle will transmute the negative intent of the energy." I pour a second trail of sea salt from the red candle to the white candle. "As it's transmuted, the energy will flow from the red candle to the white candle, making that energy pure again."

I pour a third trail, winding from the white candle, all around the cookie sheet, to a space in the far corner where I've placed the paper with my goal on it. "Then the energy that is now pure follows my trail of salt all the way to my goal to help make my intended goal possible, to help it manifest."

Rhiannon laughs. "So any of the negative stuff that Lady Dragon sends to you—"

I nod and finish her sentence. "—Is turned positive and helps to fuel my spell for extra protection."

"Cool!" both girls exclaim together as I light the black candle. Then I light the red and then the white.

The three candles burn quickly. I'd expected to wait an hour, but they're done in less than ten minutes. They've never burned so fast and hard.

As the candles burn, I send the girls to pack a suitcase so we can stay with Grandma on the farm in Georgia for a few days while we wait out the results of the hurricane. It's only a few hours away, but I don't want to repeat the catastrophic events the morning Hurricane Opal had hit in 1995 and we'd been stuck on a four-lane highway with every lane headed north and nothing moving because we'd left too late…because Quent had to visit his mommy before we fled for our lives. My instincts told me that Ivan was coming straight for us, a repeat of Opal. Hurricane Opal, coming in as a Category 5 and dropping back to a Cat 3 just before it made landfall, had still managed to wipe out a huge number of homes on the Gulf Coast, right down to the slabs—and less.

The girls pack quickly, but before they can put their suitcases and way too many stuffed animals into the Mercedes—which is too small for anything anyway—Sonnet reports back to the kitchen as I'm busily unplugging the hard drive to my computer so that at least if we lose everything else, all my books and financial information is saved.

"There's a message on the answering machine, Mommy. It's from Miss Donna. I think you need to go listen to it. Right now." Her voice cracks. She's heard something that has her alarmed.

"Here," I say, handing her one of the photograph albums of her and her sister when they were babies. "Put this in the trunk of the car for me, okay?" I pat her head and kiss her forehead as if nothing's wrong and send her on her way.

I punch the answering machine button and wait. My stomach's knotting up again. If I didn't have my Third Degree Elevation, I'm not sure how bad it would be.

"Hey." Donna's voice is strained. "Look, I've been talking to Barbara and Mariah and Jenna and some of the others and, well, we think you should evacuate. I don't have time to explain right now. We're...*I'm* on my way to Barbara's. I'm driving all the way over there. Tonight. So we can do a ritual, just for you. You'd said you welcomed any help with shielding from Dragon, so we're going to gather and send you a little extra energy. I still have your cord where we took your measure at Initiation, so we'll use that to send you some extra power. I swore when you went through your Third that I'd never let anyone come between us, but what Dragon's doing now.... I don't know." She laughs without amusement. "We may have to drop her in molasses and freeze her. Anyway, I still have some contacts left inside Dragon Hart. I heard from them today, and I don't like what I heard."

She could have been talking about Leo, but I doubt it. Even though he's clairvoyant and must certainly have seen things about her, he still adores his M'Lady Dragon and would never do anything against her as long as he's still in the Grand Coven. But Tyler, his partner? Tyler is likely the one feeding Donna information, even though Donna has never mentioned his name and she's really not one to keep that many secrets.

"Dragon's made some big changes in the past month," the voice on the tape continues. "Raven, you need to know that. She's really tightened up on the group. Demanding utter loyalty. She's also announced that she took back your Third Degree. Revoked your status. I know, I know. She's always said that whatever Spirit bestows, a mere mortal cannot take away, but she's damned sure decided to try. Oh, I know she hasn't, but she's saying she has. She's saying she took it back from you because you were intentionally deceptive and you lack integrity."

What? My teeth clench. I can't help it. Integrity's one of my hot buttons. I hadn't known for certain I'd be leaving Dragon Hart until I saw Dragon's abusive nature for what it was.

"Anyway," the recording continues, "she sent out a message and I'm sure she thinks it's going to get back to you and I guess I'm the one letting it get back to you, but the message is, you need to remember that in the old days, when a witch betrayed her coven, she was put to death. I'm not saying that to scare you but…she *is* saying it to scare you and she is doing some things that, if I were you, I'd be a little nervous about. You need to pump up your shields as much as you possibly can and be—" The message cuts off.

Donna's voice resumes in the next phone message. "Anyway, Raven, you need to use every trick in the book because, trust me, she's going to. Now, you'll be fine. Mariah's boyfriend, Payne, is a talented psychic himself and he says you're going to be okay, but I don't think you want to be in your house when Hurricane Ivan hits. Okay? You don't need to be hanging out in the living room and playing board games, he said. Give me a call when you get to your parents' house. If you can't reach me, leave a message on my machine so I'll know you're safe. Okay? Love you!"

Damn it! I pound the wall with my fist. Sonnet, walking into the room, sees the impact of my hand against the plaster and stops cold in her tracks.

"It's okay, sweetheart. Just keep putting things in the car and...do it faster. Okay?"

Damn it! Why is Dragon doing this? She is one of the most powerful witches in the country and yet she's focusing all her time and effort on *me?* Why? Because of ego? Because she's pissed that I left her group? I would have loved to have stayed in the Grand Coven, but I couldn't. There was something that made it wrong for me to do, something that made it impossible to do whatever this great mission is I'm supposed to do. I *had* to leave. I don't fully understand it yet, but I do know that I couldn't stay.

And I resent that she's wasting her time and energy on me and I resent that I didn't get a chance to really enjoy getting my Third Degree and bask in its afterglow because I've spent so much time having to shield, and I pity her, and I'm angry.

But most of all, most of all, I see all the wonderful things that she could be doing with all the energy and the power that she does have and she's wasting it over nothing!

What's wrong with all these "big" witches that they get caught up in all their petty little witch wars all the time and stuck in all their ego? It's not about them. It's about getting the word out about the God and the Goddess and about service and about helping other people spiritually.

How will non-pagans ever take us seriously if we can't get our act together? What right do we have to call ourselves spiritual if we're constantly trying to hurt each other?

And damn it, I resent the time that I'm spending shielding. There is so much other work I could be doing with that energy right now and so many better places to put my energy other than keeping Dragon's nightmares away from my children.

And she has the audacity to question my integrity? Sheesh. What else can possibly go wrong?

"Mommy?" Rhiannon gestures at me to get my attention, but she's clearly nervous. "Um, Mommy? Daddy's at the front door."

Argh! Good grief. I roll my eyes. All I have to do is ask what else can go wrong and he appears. Speak of the devil.

"Fabulous," I mutter through grated teeth.

"Something wrong?"

I startle. I'm not expecting Quent to be standing there, a few feet behind me. In *my* house. Why does he have to do that, just walk right in like that? Oh, yeah. Control.

I spin to face him. "I've decided to evacuate. It looks like Ivan's going to be a Cat 5 when it hits here."

He glares at me. "Might be nice to know where my daughters are. When were you going to tell me this?"

"Oh, about five minutes after I decided," I pop back at him. "I guess that means you're going to have to wait about three more minutes."

He looks surprised at my tone, but then he's never really heard me talk back to him before. My patience is exceedingly thin at the moment.

"Oh," he says at last. "You just decided. All right. I thought I'd come over and help you prepare for the hurricane. Batten down the hatches and what-not."

Hmmm, I think, *that would be a first, since I'm always that one who battens down the hatches.* He's never in all the years we lived her together put up plywood over the windows or taped a single glass pane or closed even one curtain. The most he's ever done has been to—

"I'll take care of getting in the lawn furniture," he offers.

"I've already handled that. Most of it, anyway. There are a couple of pieces left. A patio table and two chairs. While the girls were packing, I've already been out there to put away anything that might turn into a missile. I left those items only because I saw a wasp on the table between my trips from the back yard to the garage to put things away." I cleaned everything off the table—candles, spare firewood, everything except for a pre-packaged fire log with half the paper torn off.

Quent waves a dismissive hand as I mention the wasp again. "I'll take care of it," he says.

"The wasps," I try to warn him, but before I can say anything further, he shrugs away from me.

"Poor little wasps never hurt anybody."

There he goes again! Nothing I say has any validity with him. I can tell him something a hundred times and be dismissed a hundred times, but let his mother or his siblings or some stranger at his job tell him the same thing, and it's suddenly gospel.

As he stands in front of me, Quent doesn't look quite so familiar to me anymore. There's something about him that really is a stranger to me now. It's odd, this feeling, like I never really knew him.

Only now do I understand that I never knew him at all. There's darkness and negativity all around him. It comes off of him in waves. Yes, this is why he was so insistent regarding not moving out of the house. He knew that once I was away from his energy for a while, his control over me would fade. His presence had been like a wet blanket over my fire. The best I could do was smolder and steam and suffocate, but now the blanket has been jerked off, and I am just beginning to flame.

A part of me still wonders why I had to go through all of that with him and why I'm still going through this now, all these changes so abruptly, so fast, but there's a little voice inside my head now—a knowing—that tells me that it had to be this way, that these changes had to come this fast, because there's something very important for me to do in this world. And I can't take my time to change into the person I need to be to do what I need to do. It has to be fast. That may be hard and it may be abrupt but there's not other way it can be. It's like that Tower card, the catastrophe that shakes me to my foundation, and yet in the long run, it puts me in a much better place.

Quent pauses at the kitchen table to flip through the day's mail that the girls have left scattered across the surface. There's nothing there for him except for bills and he leaves those. He pauses at the day's paper, flips it open across the table and begins to read the front page. He reads several headlines aloud, announcements about the impending storm, and then leafs through the paper.

"Oh, look," he mimics. "There's an ad for Dr. Matthews." He folds the paper over so that the ad is showing and leaves it on the table.

I glance over his shoulder. I haven't had time to read the paper, and I won't unless I remember to take it with me on our evacuation. Dr. Matthews' clinic is advertising his services with a huge, goofy-looking picture of him—one that looks nothing like him—in a suit. He looks uncomfortable, unnatural. If he weren't wearing a tie and if the shirt had been unbuttoned at the top and his hair a bit mussed, it would have resembled the physician who always meets my girls with a bright smile and funny story and meaningful glint in the eye to reassure their mom. But there is a part of Dr. Matthews that isn't what it appears.

Beneath the black and white professional portrait are words in big block letters:

JESSE MATTHEWS, MD.

ACCEPTING

NEW PATIENTS

"I forgot to tell you," Quent says. "I had an appointment with Dr. Matthews last week."

"Really?" I try to keep my tone even. I don't want to give away that Dr. Matthews accidentally spilled the beans to me by letting me know that Quent cancelled his appointment and that Quent hasn't seen our mutual physician in quite some time.

"Yeah, uh, remember that physical I had scheduled a couple of months ago? Yeah, Dr. Matthews finally got the results back, and so I stopped in to see him and I'm fine. I'm just perfect. All my former medical problems have gone away and I've improved since then. He says my diet is perfect and I need to keep doing what I'm doing and keep playing basketball about twenty hours a week because it's ideal exercise. He says I shouldn't change a thing and it's too bad more people don't have as healthy a lifestyle as I do."

"Really. That's…great, Quent. That's really great."

He laughs. "Yeah. He did try to offer me some samples of Viagra." Quent tosses the folded paper back onto the table with Dr. Matthews' face staring back at me from grainy black and white. "Yeah, but I told him I didn't need it." Quent laughs nervously. "I didn't tell him, of course, that you and I weren't sleeping together anymore."

You didn't tell him anything, I think. *And if you had, it would have been lies.*

Both girls show up at my elbows. They stand on either side of me like little bodyguards.

"What do you want us to do now, Mommy?" Rhiannon asks.

"Go outside and take down the hummingbird feeders and anything else that might turn into flying missiles in a hurricane-force wind."

"Yes," Quent says with his usual self-importance, "and Daddy's going to go outside and take care of all the heavy furniture for you guys." He says it in a sing-songy tone and I know the girls are rolling their eyes even though I can't see them where they stand.

"Quent, you really didn't have to come over to help. I can take care of everything on my own, and what I can't do on my own, the girls can help me with."

I'm positive he hasn't thought about my knee problems and how it really is extremely difficult for me to climb up on a ladder to get hanging baskets of flowers down from their hooks. Or to get up and down from the back door to the ground because the back deck had to be replaced and having the rotten wood and steps hauled away is as far as I've gotten and it's a long and very painful step down.

He shrugs. "I'm just protecting my investment. Before our divorce is final—if you insist on going through with the divorce—this house is still half mine."

Yes. Accountant that he is, he always speaks of assets and liabilities. My income is an asset to him but my spirituality, as far as he's concerned, is a liability.

"Besides," he adds, "maybe this hurricane will blow away your roof."

"What?" I stare at him. He isn't kidding.

"Yeah. Then you can finally get it replaced."

I grind my teeth. Yes, I do need a new roof. Just as with the deck, we've needed a new roof for the past few years, but Quent refused to spend any money on it. However, since moving out of the house, he's been pestering me that if I go through with the divorce, I need to get the roof replaced because that will increase the value of the house. What he's failed to mention is that he expects me to pay for a new roof—which will run me well over $20,000 and will increase the value of the house, according to our real estate agent, by $20,000 to $30,000, and I'd have to pay him half of that amount since it would be the value of the increase in the house. So I'd be out at least $30,000 more if I put a new roof on the house before the divorce. Once again, he is finagling numbers, and I'd be on the short end of that financial stick.

Quent edges out the back door, making a snide re-mark about the lack of back steps while I give the girls fur-ther instructions. Sonnet is to go throughout the entire house and place the protection rune, *algiz*, on each of the windows with a marker that will easily wipe off later. Rhiannon is to take a piece of paper that shows the seal of an angel that protects against the winds and storms and recreate it as a chalk drawing on the driveway. Her dad will think she's playing and won't know what it is. The win-dows in the house are already taped up, though if the winds are raging at 160 miles per hour, there's not much an X of tape can do except keep the glass from shattering and scat-tering when it pops out. Later, when Quent's gone, I'll take care of the extra shielding while I have the girls close the blinds on all the windows in the house.

I follow Quentin outside. "Be careful," I tell him, "of wasps." He's been moved out for almost six weeks, and I've noticed several new nests around the premises that have been built since his absence began. I've been too busy with divorce paperwork, particularly the minutia Quent wanted me to recite back to him, to knock down the new nests. "There's a new nest near—"

"I know what I'm doing!" he yells back in a sudden angry burst as I unhook a birdfeeder to move it into an empty shed. "You don't give me credit for anything!" He stomps over to the lawn furniture, grabs both chairs, and hauls them around to the garage.

Both girls are once again at my elbows. They've heard his outburst, and they're feeling protective of me. Again.

"Sonnet will do the windows after Daddy leaves," Rhiannon tells me. "And I'll do the driveway after he leaves. We should be out here with you right now. We… we don't want you to be alone."

My eyes sting. My babies are protecting me once again. In some ways, I am still very fragile, and they know this.

Quent stomps back around to the lawn furniture. As lightly as the girls and I tend to tread in the grass, it's amazing to me that he can make so much noise. We can feel the earth shuddering under his footfalls even though he's a good fifty feet away and on the other side of the yard.

I look up just in time to see him reach for the fire log on top of the patio table where I'd spotted the wasp. Before his hand even touches the log, a brown tornado rises from the table like some demon that's been summoned. I frown and wrap my arms around the girls to keep them still and close. I've never seen anything like this. Then Quent spins and runs screaming across the yard!

Oh. Okay. It's not a brown tornado. Wasps. Wasps everywhere!

He manages to evade them without getting stung and, to his credit, he doesn't lead them to us. I guess all those hours running up and down the basketball court have been good for something!

He goes back into the house, finds the hornet spray, and then comes out and soaks both the patio table and the fire log from twelve or fifteen feet away. "I'll, uh, come back tomorrow or…or before the hurricane and, uh, I'll, uh, move that table," he says. "It can stay there for now."

He's so unnerved he can barely talk, but he leaves. Thank Gods. He leaves.

Once he's gone, the girls and I creep near the table. Not so close as to get stung or to step on a writhing wasp in the grass, but just close enough to see what Quentin found—or had found him. Just on the inside of the wrapper around the fire log is a wasp nest bigger than both my outstretched hands. Hundreds of dead wasps litter the table.

"Oooh, Mommy," Sonnet says in a trembling voice, "I'm glad you saw that wasp earlier."

"I don't believe this." Rhiannon shakes her head. "Mommy, we've used that table all summer. Especially since Daddy left and we started doing little cookouts out here. We were out here last night, all around that table. I was talking to Diana on the phone and I sat the phone down on that log when I went to get a Vanilla Coke. And one time last night, I actually sat right there—" she points to a spot beneath a few dozen wasps— "and I sat right there on the table while I was talking to her and...."

"I know. I know, Rhiannon. We've *all* been all over that table in the past few weeks, and those wasps haven't bothered us a bit." I feel weak in my knees at the thought of what might have happened. Had the wasps been there all along? Were they part of my protective shields to protect the property from outsiders? Is it possible that I had manifested them?

While the girls draw *algiz* protection runes on the window panes in erasable purple ink and decorate the driveway with the angelic seal, I unhook my braided cords from their place in the foyer where the Main Altar sits and wrap them around me. I'm already thinking ahead to the ritual work I'll be doing in a few minutes. I take a small glass urn from a shelf in the kitchen in the area I call my witch's cupboard. It's filled with bright-colored bottles of herbs, oils, and incense for specific magickal needs. I'm careful not to open the urn until I'm in the front yard, barefoot in the grass. I start at the northern corner of the property, taking out a little pinch of the power at a time and careful not to breathe it in. I scatter it along the perimeter of my property. It's a Pow-Wow tool that Beverly, one of the Elders, told me about. I've mixed equal parts black pepper, white pepper, and red pepper, all consecrated, empowered, *blessed* for the purpose of protection and in the primary colors used in Pow-Wow magick, a little secret known by many in Pennsylvania Dutch country.

I sprinkle the Pow-Wow peppers around the border of my property. I also visualize Dragon Dogs standing guard at each corner. Dragon Dogs are a thought-form suggested to me by author Edain McCoy at one of her workshops a few years ago, and they're fiercer than anything conceived in a Harry Potter movie. Each one has several heads, looking in all directions, standing guard, keeping out intruders. Especially dragons.

The girls are back in the house and filling the bathtubs so we'll have water in case of a disaster and calling their friends so they'll know we're leaving in a few minutes. I'll call Jan as soon as I get to Georgia tonight. It's almost dark outside at this moment.

I stand before my outdoor altar and face North as I cast a circle. I cast it around my entire property like a dome over some futuristic city. Instead of calling upon totem animals, Watchtowers, or angels to stand at the corners, I call upon my Sacred Dead: Granddaddy…Alva…in the East; my old friend Jim in the South; in the West, my grandmother, Emma; and in the North, Jan's mother, Gladys, who passed a few years ago. Although it is hot and humid in mid-September, I feel the coolness of their energy all around me. The Dead always feel so cold. It's the absence of energy most people call *Life*.

I call upon the angels in charge of the winds and of the waters and in charge of protecting against storms and natural disasters, upon all the spirits of this place, and upon the Dark Mother to watch over me and mine, to keep us safe, to keep this place I call home safe. When I'm done, I leave the circle cast.

"Mommy! Mommy!" Sonnet runs out of the house and flings her arms around my waist. Her hair is damp at the forehead from all her hard work. "I was just watching The Weather Channel. They're saying now it's definitely gonna be a Cat 5, and it's coming right in here after us. They're saying that the landfall is going to be five miles from us." Her voice shakes. "Is it going to get us if we go to Grandma's, too?"

"No, sweetie," I tell her. "It's not going to get us. Now get your sister and the two of you get in the car. We leave in five minutes."

They take their last-minute bathroom breaks while I do one last walk-through of the house and pull the switches at the breaker box to prevent a fire in case of excessive damage. I then walk quickly to every large pine in the front and back yard and place my hand on the trunk of each with a command: "Withhold!" I give the command a last time to the largest pine, the one directly in front of the house, the one my dad backed into on his sole trip to our house ten years ago. I'm more worried about it than any other because if it falls, it will bisect the house, right through the living room. If it falls, it must cross the angelic seal Rhiannon has drawn in bright shades of chalk on the driveway as well as several secondary symbols, representing the house as being guarded by a Third Degree witch and that any who interfere or intrude will be beaten.

Something here will be sacrificed. I know it. I just don't know what yet or how much. But there's a sense of sacrifice needed to preserve the balance of what we won't lose.

Once the girls are in the car with my keys and purse, I walk back to the threshold of the house and, inside, pause at my Main Altar.   The mirror wards are still there, set against Dragon and her friends.   Notices of I.R.S. fraud fines and punishments are still tacked up as a reminder to Dragon if she should astral in.   Fresh-cut roses from my garden, a gift to The Morrigan, are there also.   I close my eyes for a moment, holding out my palms on either side, and feel the energies passing through me.   My hands tingle and vibrate.   I'm scared.   I can't let the girls know, but I really am scared.   My life has been so turned upside down in the past few years and now that I'm striking out on my own, the last thing I need is to find my house destroyed when I return.

I don't mind starting over.   I've wanted to start over.   But I really don't want to have to start from scratch. I need a little peace in my life right now.   A little less worry, a little less stress.   I open my eyes and cast one last look over my shoulder at my altar as I put my hand on the door to leave.

"Spirits of this place," I call out as loudly as I can, "watch over this place while I'm gone.   Keep it protected. Let there be no damage, and if must be damage, only slight."   I pause and smile, then walk out with a sense that I'm leaving both Granddaddy and my spirit guides behind.

10

Saturday - Moon in Scorpio, Waxing Crescent

Thirty miles from home—or where I hope home still is—and I'm sick to my stomach. It's been three days since the hurricane, and I finally heard this morning that the roads and bridges are clear enough for me to start heading back. I do understand why they say *clear enough* because I've already lost count of how many huge pines have fallen across the roads and bridges and someone's come along with a chain saw and lopped off the trees a few inches from the highway and left the stub there in an abrupt salute to those who might pass while the rest of each tree lies pushed into a ditch full of stagnant water. Interstate 10 was clear but too slow-moving in places, so I've taken to the back roads to get us home. They're a little dicier, but I actually feel safer.

Rhiannon sits in the front seat next to me, and Sonnet in the back. Neither of them has said anything for the past hundred miles. One county away from home, and the gas stations are already shut down, out of fuel. The only one we saw with any gas at all had a line of cars stretching for nearly a mile in either direction down Highway 90. By the time I get home—if we can get home—I'll still have half a tank of gas. It may be the only fuel I have for the next week.

But we have water with us in the trunk and canned food with a hand-crank can opener. And cash. The girls and I are safe. My parents on the farm are safe, in spite of tornadoes spun off by the outer bands of the hurricane, twisters that came within five miles of their homestead, which I'd erected yet another circle of protection.

But as for home, we've had no word. Even the on-site reporters from The Weather Channel haven't ventured out yet to see all the damage. From the looks of the aerial photography I've seen, Ivan was just as bad as Hurricane Opal or worse, even if it did drop back to a Cat 3 just before landfall. I remember reading in the mid-1990's about all the coming Earth changes—earthquakes, hurricanes, tsunamis—and that things on the planet were about to get a lot worse.

By the time we reach Highway 285, the hypnotically long, two-lane road that meanders twenty miles through Air Force forests and fields before depositing us within easy reach of home, my heart sinks. I see a police car blocking the road south.

"Oh, no," I tell the girls. I don't mean to alarm them, but it just seeps out. "All the roads home are closed. We're not going to be able to make it home today."

Almost as soon as I say it, a bulldozer crawls up behind the police car. The driver leans out and gives a thumbs-up sign. I roll down my window and lean out as if doing so would give me a better look. The policeman pulls his car into the median and then gets out. He walks forward and picks up a couple of orange security cones before stopping by my car window.

"Road's just opening up, ma'am. You can go on through now. Y'all be careful and—" he pauses and refuses to look me in the eye— "I hope you find everything at home all safe and sound."

As many times as I've been down this road, I don't recognize it. Except by my odometer, I have no idea how far I am from home or how far I've driven.

"Mommy, you're on the wrong road," Sonnet says, her voice trembling. "This isn't the way home. There used to be trees here."

"The trees are still here," I tell her. "You see those bushes out there and shrubs everywhere? Well, they're not bushes and shrubs."

I look in the mirror and see her eyes grow wide with understanding. The hurricane winds mowed down the trees in places. All that's left are the limbs of the leafy branches of the tall pines, the limbs sticking straight up now. Like man-high shrubs.

The closer we get to home, the more severe the destruction becomes. Closer to home, we see steeples torn off churches, tin roofs missing from barns, the signs gone, trees down, and even a couple of sailboats that have washed from the bayou across the street and into someone's front yard.

The traffic moves gingerly toward the community where I live, but it *does* move and the bridge isn't out. I am hopeful, so hopeful.

As I turn onto the road in my neighborhood, my heart plummets. The tension in the car is palpable. Both girls are sitting stiff and upright, staring out the window at everything. It's hard to tell where to turn onto the street I live on.

I miss the turn. How did I miss the turn?

Dodging piles of debris, I do a u-turn and go back and find it this time, right where it's always been. The big oak trees on either side of the street, however, are gone— replaced by towers of sawed-up oak stumps, piled onto the roadside.

My house isn't far down the street, but it takes forever to reach. When I round the corner, the first thing I see is the big tree in our front yard…on top of the house. The girls and I gasp at the same time. I can't pull into the driveway. The heavy tree trunk crosses it diagonally, leaning across the top of the house right over the threshold, right over the living room where we would have been if we had stayed.

"Please, Gods," I beg, "don't let it have gone through."

Right over the threshold to my home. Right over the Main Altar. I've seen pines not nearly as big as this one that have crashed all the way through the house to the foundation. But this one…it's the oddest thing.

The girls and I stand in the driveway and stare at it. Rhiannon races back to get the digital camera we left in the trunk along with the other computer equipment. She starts snapping pictures of the tree, of the roof. She walks backward to the street and snaps several pictures of the whole house. On her way back, she steps barefoot on a big green pinecone buried up in the grass like a Department of Defense projectile and howls at the small cuts it leaves on her sole.

There are little limbs along the driveway, too, and some branches that are almost the diameter of my wrist. The yards are a mess, full of trash that's blown in from other yards, including several kinds of shingles and cancelled checks bearing an address at the beach five miles away. And broken limbs from the thirty-odd trees that encircle our house.

With the exception of the one on our roof, no trees are down in our yard. The fences are still standing. I peer across the street at my neighbor's house—the roof is gone. Half the street in front of my house is covered with limbs, and the other with at least four or five different shingles from four or five different houses. There's a piece of tin wrapped like a mummy around the trunk of the tall pine standing in my neighbor's yard. It's the only tree they have that's still standing.

A little farther down the street, several pines have fallen on another house, two destroying the entrance and another bisecting their living room. There's the oddest smell in the air. Like sawdust and sap of freshly broken pines and the swampy scent of rainwater that's been standing too long and has already stagnated to the point of attracting mosquito larvae.

I hear chainsaws in the distance, coming from all directions. An odd symphony forced together.

Many of the houses have their front doors wide open. Neighbors are waving to each other, helping each other with the damage, helping each other saw down trees and saw apart trees and take trees off roofs and pull blue tarps over what's left of other roofs.

The best I can tell, our whole neighborhood is without electricity. I sigh and think of the freezer of food rotting inside my house and wonder what put-them-in-the-freezer-to-stop-them spells might have thawed out. I do believe I have Dragon and her cronies safely frozen in an ice cube.

I hand the house keys to Sonnet. "Go open the garage," I tell her.

But instead of going inside, she presses the garage door opener on the inside of the car. And to my surprise, the door opens. We have electricity. *We have electricity.* Maybe no one else in my neighborhood, but *we* have it.

The girls help me get the ladder out, and I climb up eye level with the roof, my wounded knee screaming the whole way.

Another surprise is waiting for me on the roof. For as big as this fallen tree is, as hard as its branches are that hit the roof, not a one of the big limbs punched through. In fact, there's no damage at all to the roof except for a single missing shingle. That's it. I look underneath the tree branches against the roof and realize they're barely touching. The tree itself didn't crash through my house. Even though its trunk is as big as my embrace. No, it simply leaned over *very…very…very* gently, popped at the base, but did not even press hard against the edge of the roofline. The maximum damage is a half-inch dent where the tree had leaned against the edge of the roof…and a missing shingle.

I climb down from the ladder, knees still aching. I'm incredulous. The tree simply leaned over gently against my roof and snapped at the base when it could so easily have crashed right through my living room!

"What's wrong, Mommy?" Sonnet asks. The girls fear the worst.

"We've been blessed, baby-doll. That's what's right, not what's wrong. We've been blessed."

We walk through the house to check it out. I find a few tiny leaks in the corner of one room. Circles no bigger then quarters where the hurricane winds forced water under the flashing around the front entrance. The damage to the house is nil.

True, I still have a tree to get off my roof, but the fact that a pine tree so big that I can't fit my arms around it just oh-so-gently leaned across my roof and snapped at the base, well, I'm just amazed. I shouldn't be, I know. It's exactly what I asked for. A sacrifice if need be, yes, but such a small one. And as soon as I have a chance to check out the rest of the property, I intend to conduct a gratitude ritual.

I open my freezer, expecting a stench. But everything seems to be okay. Even the ice cubes containing Dragon and company haven't melted and refrozen. According to the flashing clock, we lost electricity for only two or three hours. Probably the only ones in the neighborhood who have it back.

We open the blinds and the curtains and raise the windows and prance around the house, happy that we have a house. We're sad for the destruction we've seen around us, but we're so overcome by gratitude that we can't help ourselves. The three of us are absolutely giddy with thankfulness.

The phone rings, and Sonnet snatches it up before I can get to it. She holds it out to me. "It's for you. It's Donna."

I take the phone with a grin. "You knew I just got home, didn't you?"

She laughs, but it's a hollow laugh. "Yeah, I knew it was about time. Well, how did you do? Are you okay?"

"We're okay. The house is okay, too." I explain about the tree on the roof.

"Looks like your shields held. Congratulations. We were sending you energy, too. Just about all we've been doing has been to send you energy so you could be protected. I told you, I will always keep you safe from Dragon. You swore your oath to me at your Third Degree Elevation and you will always be mine to protect. I'm glad things turned out well for you. We did it. We did. Using every powerhouse spell we knew, and trying to reinforce those shields for you."

"Well, I guess it worked. We're in far better shape than anyone else around here. I have a feeling we'll be having some neighborhood cookouts over here as well. The good thing about disasters like this is it does bring out the best in everyone."

"Hmm," she says. "The worst, too."

"What do you mean?"

"Raven, I was calling to see if you needed me to fly down there and help you dig out or anything. I've been watching the news, and it looks pretty bad in Pensacola. I know that's an hour away from you."

"Yeah, I've heard those reports, too. Homes that are completely gone, foundation and all. But we're okay here. Please don't worry about me."

"Okay. Good to know. In that case, I have to go help Barbara and Mariah and—"

"What's happened?"

"The remnants of Hurricane Ivan happened. After the winds calmed down, the rains continued and that storm system came right up from where you are in Florida, came right up the East Coast. It won't stop raining. My basement's flooded. Jenna's home is...well, it's gone. Beverly lives on the Delaware River and the water's up to the second story of her house. Barbara's got a little flood damage but not much. Mainly damage to her barns. Mariah's car, last she saw it, was upside down in the parking lot where she works and under six feet of water."

"What?"

She mentions the names of two or three other Elders and members who left Dragon Hart recently, all of whom suffered damage from Hurricane Ivan and its aftermath. All of the damages far more significant than mine.

"Raven, I'm leaving in about five minutes. I have to get the dogs boarded and then I'm out of here. The neighbors are going to take care of my basement for me. But if you're sure you don't need me—"

"I'm sure, Donna. Are you sure *you* don't need *me?*"

"No, no, I'll be fine. But Barbara and the others... Jenna especially.... You know I think Dragon was madder at her than anyone else."

"You think Dragon did all this?"

"I don't know. Like I said before, she has a way of manifesting things. She doesn't necessarily know how it's going to manifest, but she puts out that energy and she aims it directly at her enemies. You beat her this time. Your shields were stronger."

"We beat her," I correct. "And beating her wasn't really the intent. My intent was to just live my life without her bothering me, you know? Can't she find something better to do with all that energy?"

"One would think so, Raven. In any case, I think she'll leave you alone for a while. She saw your history with your ex-husband and she underestimated you. She saw how quiet you could be and she underestimated you. She thought you were going to be a pushover. I think Dragon got surprised."

"Donna, I just want to be left alone, you know? I want Quent to leave me alone so I can start my new life, and I want Dragon to leave me alone so I can start my new life. I'm eager to get my new circle started. It's something we talked about for the past year, and it looks like finally it's going to happen. Everything in my life has been falling into place. The Goddess has this great plan for me and this mission for me. I still don't know what it is yet, but I know it's coming. And I'm just so ready to get on with my life."

"More power to you, girl. You do it. Meanwhile, I'm off and running, and I'll call you in a few days and let you know how Jenna's doing and Beverly and Mariah and the rest of the group."

Even before I hang up, I can't stop thinking of the other Elders. It could so easily have been me without a place to lay my head, instead of talking from the comfort of my home where I have electricity. I could just as easily been walking through rubble.

I hang up. The message light flashes. One new message. I sigh. Probably Quent calling to check on the girls to make sure we're back and make sure we're okay. I haven't called him yet, and the girls haven't mentioned it. Sadly, they're just not that eager to see him. I punch the button and wait, but it isn't Quent's voice.

"Hey, Lauren. This is Lisa. Just wanted to let you know we're all right. Just some trees down and some fences and no electricity. I'm calling from a pay phone so you won't be able to reach me. Anyway I just wanted to let you know that, um, I know you were wanting to get together this month to get the circle started, but work's crazy right now, especially with all the hurricane victims around here. And it's going to be at least a few more weeks before I can even think about it."

Her voice pauses, then bursts forth in a crackle of sound. "Oh, and one more thing: that guy I was going to introduce you to...you know the one who is a widow with children? You asked me if he plays guitar because you thought he would be this guy you're supposed to meet. I saw him earlier in the week, right before Hurricane Ivan hit, and the answer is yes, he does play guitar. As a matter of fact, he teaches guitar, but he's not as young as I thought. I don't know if that matters to you. He's actually in his forties. He just looks a lot younger. Anyway, I'll introduce you sometime. I have a feeling he may be your Treat."

In his forties? Leo had said The Treat was younger. Maybe Leo was seeing The Treat as he looked years ago.

I grimace as the answering machine clicks off. I don't have time for The Treat right now. I just want to get my life in order. I just want to get this divorce over and feel happy again. I want joy in my life, more than anything right now. I want to feel joy again. Maybe later, I'll find a man who will accept me as I am, but for now, finding joy is enough.

It's coming, echoes in my head.

He's coming, another echo says.

I think the first voice was Granddaddy's. But this one is feminine, and I don't recognize it.

And then a third voice, one that radiates power, says, *They're coming.*

I try to phone Jan but get no answer. She loses her electricity in every storm, so I'm not panicked.

I leave the girls inside to call their friends and check their status while I head outside, tying my cords around me as I go. I use the janitorial broom I keep in the garage to sweep the driveway clean of green pine needles and small oak limbs and hard green pinecones everywhere just waiting to cut our bare feet as they already have Rhiannon's.

I duck underneath the tree and pat its felled trunk. The symbols and the seals on the driveway are all gone now, blasted clean by the rain. Where the tree fell, or rather gently leaned against the house, was directly over the spot where I performed my shielding ritual. It's time for me to release my circle of protection meant to keep us safe from this hurricane.

But I'll leave my wards in place. Dragon is still out there, unsuccessful in her attempts right now, but still there. Still focused on her witch war against me and against the former Elders of Dragon Hart.

Before I can even ground and center, I hear Sonnet scream. My heart freezes. *What now?* Mentally I'm already there with her, faster than my feet will travel. I bolt back into the house, through the living room, through the kitchen, out the backdoor. I'm in midair before I remember that we haven't had steps in two years and that I'm waiting for the repair man to come rebuild the back deck.

"It's okay," Sonnet calls back. "I was on the phone with my friend and I saw the snake and it's gone now. But it's okay."

I land on the hard ground, my right knee buckling under me. I come down hard on my knee, bending it sideways as I fall. The pain is excruciating. I yelp, but I don't even recognize my own voice. I can't move. It hurts too much. It even overwhelms the instinct of getting to my baby and the snake. Sonnet and Rhiannon are both at my side, asking if I'm okay. I can barely hear them through the throbbing in my knee.

"Snake?" I manage to squeak at Sonnet.

"It's okay, Mommy. He's gone."

"It's only a grass snake," Rhiannon tells me. "The hurricane probably ran it out of its home. Either that or the water put it—oh, Mommy, are you okay?"

I'm crying hard. They don't usually see me cry. They saw enough of my tears over their dad, even when I tried to hide them. This time the pain isn't emotional but physical. And they're at a loss for what to do.

"I'll get you some ice water," Sonnet offers and disappears. Somehow, she thinks ice water always makes everything better.

A few minutes later, after the slightly dulling sensation of pain, I hear her running back through the house, bare feet pounding on the floor, ice cubes jingling against the glass. She reappears at my side and thrusts the glass at my face. I want to hug my knee, I want to hold it, I want to press into it, restrain the pain. But instead I reach for the glass and take a sip. She beams back at me, happy to be of help.

Rhiannon's a little more mature and worried in a different way. A frown knits her otherwise smooth forehead. "Do I need to take you to the doctor? I could probably get a neighbor to drive you. I can't drive yet," she reminds me. "I'm only 14."

I shake my head. "I don't know yet." Besides, it's Saturday and Dr. Matthews' clinic isn't open on Saturdays.

All the work I've done in physical therapy to build my knees back up, to keep the swelling down, all the work I've done, and now in one single movement I've undone it all. I've been willing to accept that this knee problem was for some greater good and I told myself that it was so I could stay home and plan to launch a new career. And then I told myself it's also to take care of my divorce paperwork. And then over the past few days, I told myself that it was to take care of hurricane matters.

But now, oh Gods, what now?

When I can finally stop crying, the girls help me inside the house and put me on the sofa. Sonnet brings me two blankets. It's way too hot for either, but I take them anyway, put them under my knee and elevate it, but I can't stop hugging my knee. I need the pressure of my hands against the pain.

"What do you want us to do?" Rhiannon asks, pushing the glass of ice water in my direction. I take a sip and then press the cold glass to my knee. It feels a little better. "Do you need a doctor?"

"Oh!" Sonnet cries out and scrambles away.

"Or I can call an ambulance," Rhiannon suggests. "I know they're supposed to be expensive, but maybe I can see if a neighbor can just drive you to the emergency room."

"No." I shake my head. "No, it's not broken, but I may have strained it again. Maybe tore something. We'll just have to wait and see."

I hear the ripping of paper and wonder what Sonnet's up to now. She runs back to me and thrusts a newspaper ad in my face so close to my eyes that I can't read it. I pull back and focus. It's the ad for Dr. Matthews. He's their physician, too. She's torn the ad so that just his goofy-looking portrait shows with the words under it:

JESSE MATTHEWS, MD.

ACCEPTING

"Thanks, sweetie, but it's okay." Though I know without a doubt that I'll have to see Dr. Matthews again and have him take a look at it. I wasn't planning on having to go back to him, but I guess now I have no choice.

She opens a hardback book on the coffee table, one I've been reading, *The Elegant Universe,* which is about string theory and quantum physics, and she slips the newspaper ad inside where my bookmark is. She replaces it on the table.

"Maybe I should call Auntie Jan," Sonnet suggests. "She'll know what to do."

"It's okay, Sonnet. I know what to do. I'll be fine. I'll report back to physical therapy tomorrow and talk to Cindie about it. Until then, we watch it and see if my knee swells up like a tree trunk again. Right now, there's not a lot I can do for it except to stay off it and, well, I might put an ice pack on it in a few minutes."

"Oh!" Sonnet jumps up and runs for the refrigerator ice bin. And sure enough, within ten seconds I hear the clinking of ice into a Ziploc bag. She brings it back and presses it against my knee.

"Thank you, sweetie," I say.

Rhiannon bites her lip and looks around the room, then suddenly remembers something as if it will make me feel better and take away my pain. "Oh, I took pictures of all the damage around the house. Want to see?"

I nod yes, and she and her sister simultaneously scramble for the camera. With a triumphant glare at Sonnet, Rhiannon wins. She flips through the pictures. One after another, artistically done. She has a gift for photography. She's wasted several shots on odd-shaped pine cones burrowed into the grass like little missiles. Then other shots of leaves and limbs, and finally pictures of the house from a distance and of the tree leaning against the house.

"Oh," she says and cocks her head. "Who is the man looking at the house with you?"

"What?"

"Right there." She points to the tiny screen. "There's a man standing beside you. I didn't hear him come up. I didn't see him then. Is he a neighbor?"

I don't answer. I take the camera from her. I magnify the image. She's right. There *is* a man standing behind me while I'm looking at the tree on the house. He has his back to the camera, and I can't see his face. There's something familiar about his silhouette, but I can't place it. I didn't realize there was anyone there with me.

"I-I don't know. There wasn't anyone there. No one came up while we were at the house." I'm stumped.

"It's not Daddy, is it?" Sonnet asks, crossing her arms.

"No, it's definitely not Daddy. This man's hardly any taller than I am. And he's...he's older."

I forward through the pictures, clicking one after another. He's not in the next frame or the one after that or the one after that. I go back to the earlier pictures of the house and magnify each one.

"There he is again." Rhiannon points to a shadow on the window of Sonnet's room. "You're standing over here, but there's a shadow in the glass."

"It's not my shadow," I say. "See, here's my shadow at my feet."

"But Mommy, it's *somebody's* shadow."

I magnify the image again and then one more time. *Gods.* It's not a shadow. It's a *person* in the window. Inside Sonnet's room. He's peering out. It's not a reflection of anything from the street or from the fallen tree. No, I can see reflections of things in the street. I can see the reflection of the mailbox, of the tree. I can see my own shadow's reflection in the window. And then there's this image that isn't a reflection of anything. It's just...there. It's a man, an older man with a hat on.

Sonnet nuzzles her head between Rhiannon's and mine and peers into the screen. "What's that man doing in my room, Mommy? Who is that?"

I magnify one last time, the most I can possibly magnify. The resolution doesn't get any better and the camera won't focus any further into the picture. But it doesn't need to. I recognize the man now. An older man, probably in his seventies, short and slender, and as fiercely protective as any warrior.

"It's Granddaddy," I say. "It's Alva."

"What's he doing inside my room?" Sonnet asks.

"And outside," Rhiannon reminds her.

"Well, girls, I guess he's here because I asked him to be here. I asked him to stay and protect this place for us." I sniff back the tears.

Sonnet adjusts the ice pack on my knee, but it's not my knee that hurts. Right now it's my heart. Granddaddy's been dead for nine years, and sometimes I really miss him. I wish I'd had more time to talk to him when he was alive, but he was hard of hearing and I was soft of voice. And I wasted way too much time. He'd been fifty-nine years older than I was, and I'd thought that we had nothing in common. Yet now he is with me all the time, watching after me and watching after my girls.

"I have something I have to do," I announce to the girls as I pull myself up off the sofa. "I want you both to stay here."

I half-limp, half-hop out onto the driveway to where the tree lies across the house, to where I stood to cast my circle. The girls stay behind and fret. They want to come, too, but I explain that this is something I have to do by myself.

I stand in my circle, mostly on one leg, favoring my newest injury, and I give thanks to The Morrigan for protecting me, and to the angels, and to my Sacred Dead—Granddaddy, Jim, Grandma, and Jan's mom. I bless them all with heartfelt gratitude, for blessing me with their presence and their help.

I feel the energy surging through me like a wildfire overtaking a dry pasture. It comes up through my feet, out through my head and hands, it comes down from the sky into my crown chakra, into the top of my head and down into my feet and into the concrete driveway beneath my soles.

I fling my arms skyward. *This I know is what it feels like to be a Third Degree High Priestess!* It feels like being reborn.

Getting my Third Degree wasn't the end or the culmination but rather, the launching pad to the future. The Tower card that shook me to my foundation is now a Tower that I can climb to greater heights.

There's a reason for all of this. It's all part of a divine plan. A reason for all the pain I went through with Quent. A reason now for this re-injury to my throbbing knee. And for whatever reason that my knees were paining me to begin with. I guess the work to be done with them and because of them is not yet over.

There's a new life ahead of me, a new mission, a new plan. This is starting over, starting fresh, starting from a place of love, both for myself and for others. A place of respecting myself enough to take care of myself now.

Except for a few words of prophecy that I've heard from Leo and some of the Elders, I really don't know what's ahead of me. I know I was born to do something important, though. Even if no one knows my name... because it's not my name that's important but what I have to do. It's the work that has to be done.

And this is just the beginning. There's so much to come. And I know in my heart that it's going to come hard and it's going to come fast. The pain, tragedy, and finally, *finally* joy, and according to Leo, even love with a real Treat of a man.

As I close my circle and send its energy deep into the ground, I remember Leo's prophecy.

"The Gods love you so much that They're willing to strip away from you everything that is illusion and replace it with something that's real."

I'm not sure if the "something real" is simply a wonderful new man coming into my life or if it's absolutely everything in my life. But I'm ready, Gods.

I'm ready!

Highly recommended:

"The Advanced Bonewits' Cult Danger Evaluation Frame," http://www.neopagan.net

Coming Next...

A Wedding of Souls
Spiritual Unions, Dreams,
Scientific Theory of Magick

Lauren has qualms about performing her first wedding ritual—which will damn the lovers--but follows where the Goddess leads...straight to the truth about Jesse's disappearance.

A sneak peek at *A Wedding of Souls*, flash-forwarding 15 months into the lives of Lauren, Jesse, Jan, Donna, Rhiannon, and Sonnet ... .

Something's coming. Something important.

My third chakra's doing flip-flops. I can't shake this antsy feeling, this edginess that crawls up my spine. It's almost like an anxiety attack.

I had a few of those when I was married to Quent. Usually when he was insisting I give up my spirituality or he'd leave me. Still trying to make me choose between my lifelong dream and our marriage.

But I don't get stressed like that anymore. Not in that way. When I do feel stress, it's rare. And it feels great not to have to deal with chest pains every day of my life or constantly downing Ibuprofens to get rid of yet another headache.

Sometimes I do feel my vibrations increase. Almost like the Higher Power has this dial and turns up the frequency signal. It feels almost hormonal, but it isn't. I'm in tune with something, tapped into something. Whether it's Jesse far, far away or my kids or shifts in the time-space continuum, I have no idea. But I'm tapped in and I feel it in the soles of my feet to the hair on the top of my head.

This morning, two days after Christmas and a pleasant week or so of Yule festivities, I awoke with a sense of anticipation. Almost to the point of dread.

Not that I think there's something bad coming. Actually, it feels like something good. It's just a feeling that something's coming, something major. Something soon, like in the next week.

Whatever it is, I don't think it's going to happen today, but definitely by tomorrow. Something is being set in motion.

And something will certainly have happened within the next week. Something life-altering.

Of course, I don't know what it is. It's that hidden knowledge, occult knowledge. The Moon of the Tarot deck. I don't know what it is or who it is or how it is. The only thing I know is that *something's coming. Something is about to be revealed.*

Not job-related. Not profession-based. Though I'd love to ditch my day job, it just doesn't look like that's going to happen any time soon in spite of what my personal Obi-Wan Kenobi, my very psychic friend Davinee, has said about an impending change in jobs and homes this Spring.

This feels much more personal, which is why I have to wonder if this is related to Jesse.

Ah, Jess, I miss you. So much. Where are you? And why don't you call?

In any case, whatever's coming is definitely related to Spirit and to my destiny. I sigh. Yeah, I'd love to think it's Jesse. I'd love to think that maybe in the next twenty-four hours, he's going to call me and say, "Hey, Cowgirl, I'm back in town for the weekend after spending more time than planned on a humanitarian mission in Central

America and can we go out? And hey, can I talk to your Wiccan ass about the future, and what you see, and whether we'll ever be together physically?"

But I refuse to think too much about it, refuse to get my hopes up. We've been down that road too many times before. I'm still burning candles for him. One in the ceramic pyramid for *unconditional love* with his name and birth date and birth time, the moment of his incarnation into this lifetime, scrawled in purple ink at the bottom of the candle.

I've burned these candles for him practically every night for almost nine months. And with each one I send out to him my unconditional love, in spite of what's happened between us. Or what hasn't happened between us. I still love him, and I know from deep in my heart and from my spirit guides that I also have not been forgotten.

I've been burning another candle for him, too. For most of the month of December, with the purpose of it being for us to reconnect with joy. I miss his smell. I miss his laugh. I miss his wit. I miss his eyes. I miss his face. I miss *him*. Desperately.

But our relationship is a secret one. Perhaps most of all from each other.

And what I've been told is to be, has not been. At least not in conventional ways.

A large rosebud candle that I've been burning for him since September is almost done. It's not a love spell, but rather a focus of energy. Though I may wish for it and I may hope for it, I ask for nothing in return. I simply, by burning these candles, send out my affection for him, for the Highest Good. A sweet and gentle love to let him know that I still desire his company on any plane, be it astral or earthly, and though we visit frequently in the Dreamtime, here in the physical, I haven't heard from him in over three months and I haven't seen him in six. Honestly, I'm worried.

Coming Soon...

Drink of Me
Visions, Rituals for Clarity, Healing, and Prosperity, Scientific Theory of Magick

Lauren reconnects with a lost love, who may or may not be the much prophesied new man in her life. He shares an interesting theory on magick and science and then offers her a most unexpected proposal. Will their one-on-one ritual for clarity and prosperity show Lauren the truth? Or is true love only an illusion?

A sneak peek at *Drink of Me,* returning to the story of how Lauren finds her "Treat." following the events of *Celebrating the Tower Card....*

"Your inner Aphrodite is about to emerge," Leo had told me.

I'd forgotten that he said that, that time when he first told me about The Treat. I'd responded by telling him that my inner Aphrodite was dead and buried.

"Then," he'd said, "your inner Aphrodite is about to be resurrected."

Sometimes I wonder if love really is an illusion. If it's real, I'm not even sure I know what it looks like.

Things are manifesting, yes, but so terribly slowly. Leo, one of the most talented psychics in the United States and my friend, had once told me that the Gods love me so much that they were willing to strip away everything that was illusion in my life and replace it with something real.

That was a little over a year ago and the past year has been full of having things stripped away. I'm still waiting for the replacement with something real.

So a year and six weeks after that prognostication, here I sit forcing myself to do 140-pound leg presses in the gym where I take physical therapy for my injured knees.

And in the middle of a bitter divorce. I may lose my house, but I don't think I'll lose my kids, unless my ex decides to play the religion card.

I'm also a brand new High Priestess, with my Third Degree Elevation as of six weeks ago.

And as of six weeks ago minus a few hours, I've left my Grand Coven. Over an issue with my coven leader.

Rumor has it, I was kicked out over an integrity issue, but I never lied. All I did was follow what the Gods showed me to do, and now here I am on my own.

I have no idea what the next step is, except that, well, something's manifesting.

Manifesting is a verb that's in the present tense. It hasn't manifest*ed*, it's manifest*ing,* and that means it's not done yet. It means it's brewing or it's fermenting or still working.

It's magick, whatever it is, this thing that's happening. The magick isn't generally a snap of the fingers or a twitch of the nose.

No, magick is usually subtle. Gradual.

And me, I'm impatient as hell.

Also planned for the series….

Printed in the United States
64231LVS00005B/301-327